EYEWITNESS

OCEAN

Sea slug

Red seaweed

Lesser
octopus

Cuttlefish

Fishing
trawler

Masked crab

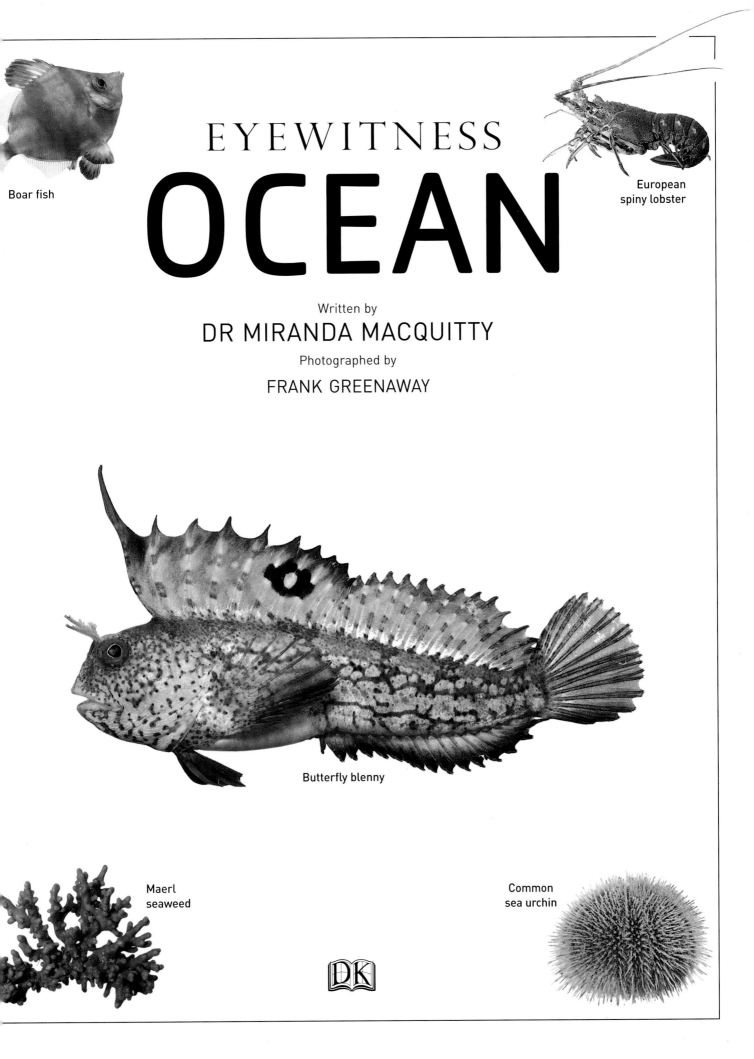

Boar fish

European
spiny lobster

EYEWITNESS
OCEAN

Written by
DR MIRANDA MACQUITTY

Photographed by
FRANK GREENAWAY

Butterfly blenny

Maerl
seaweed

Common
sea urchin

DK

Common
starfish

Red
cushion
star

DK

LONDON, NEW YORK,
MELBOURNE, MUNICH, AND DELHI

Parchment
worm inside
its tube

Project editor Marion Dent
Art editor Jane Tetzlaff
Managing editor Gillian Denton
Managing art editor Julia Harris
Research Céline Carez
Picture research Kathy Lockley
Production Catherine Semark
Special thanks The University Marine Biological
Station (Scotland) and Sea Life Centres (UK)

RELAUNCH EDITION (DK UK)
Editor Ashwin Khurana
Senior designers Rachael Grady, Spencer Holbrook
Managing editor Gareth Jones
Managing art editor Philip Letsu
Publisher Andrew Macintyre
Producer, pre-production Adam Stoneham
Senior producer Charlotte Cade
Jacket editor Maud Whatley
Jacket designer Laura Brim
Jacket design development manager Sophia MTT
Publishing director Jonathan Metcalf
Associate publishing director Liz Wheeler
Art director Phil Ormerod

RELAUNCH EDITION (DK INDIA)
Editor Surbhi Nayyar Kapoor
Art editors Deep Shikha Walia, Vikas Chauhan
Senior DTP designer Harish Aggarwal
DTP designers Anita Yadav, Pawan Kumar
Managing editor Alka Thakur Hazarika
Managing art editor Romi Chakraborty
CTS manager Balwant Singh
Jacket editorial manager Saloni Talwar
Jacket designers Govind Mittal, Suhita Dharamjit, Vidit Vashisht

This Eyewitness ® Guide has been conceived by
Dorling Kindersley Limited and Editions Gallimard

First published in Great Britain in 1995
This relaunch edition published in 2014 by
Dorling Kindersley Limited, 80 Strand, London WC2R 0RL

Copyright © 1995, © 2003, © 2008, © 2014
Dorling Kindersley Limited
A Penguin Random House Company
2 4 6 8 10 9 7 5 3 1
196429 – 07/14

A CIP catalogue record for this book is
available from the British Library.

ISBN 978-1-4093-4375-2

Colour reproduction by Alta Image Ltd, London, UK
Printed and bound by South China Printing Co Ltd, China

Discover more at

www.dk.com

Mussel shells

Red
cushion
star

Preserving
jar containing
a Norwegian
lobster

Victorian
collection
of shells

Microscope used in
the late 1800s

Prepared slides

Common sunstar

Dead man's fingers

Contents

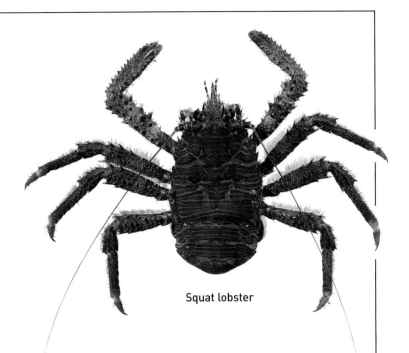

Squat lobster

Oceans of the past	6		Deep heat	46
Oceans today	8		Diverse divers	48
Ocean life	10		Submarines	50
Waves and weather	12		Ocean explorers	52
Sandy and muddy	14		Wrecks on the sea bed	54
Soft sea bed	16		Harvesting fish	56
Rocks underwater	18		Ocean products	58
On the rocks	20		Oil and gas	60
The coral kingdom	22		Oceans in peril	62
Life on a coral reef	24		Did you know?	64
Sea meadows	26		The world's oceans	66
Predators	28		Find out more	68
Homes and hiding	30		Glossary	70
Attack and defence	32		Index	72
The jet set	34			
Moving along	36			
Ocean travellers	38			
The twilight zone	40			
The darkest depths	42			
On the bottom	44			

Oceans of the past

Today's oceans started to take shape in the last 200 million years of Earth's 4,600-million-year existence. But long before, as the early planet cooled, water vapour in the atmosphere condensed, clouds formed, and rain filled the oceans. Water also came from space, in icy comets. As the land masses drifted, new oceans opened up, old oceans disappeared, and ocean life changed too. Simple organisms first appeared in the oceans 3,500 million years ago, followed by ever more complex life forms.

Spine

Ridged scale

Topsy turvy world

Wiwaxia lived on the sea floor 530 million years ago, yet this fossil was found high above sea level in Canada's Rocky Mountains. Land formed under the sea was forced up to create mountain chains.

Strong belly ribs protected under-side of bulky, rounded body

Short tail relative to total body length

Femur, or thigh bone, articulated with pelvic girdle

Huge, long, flat flipper made up of five rows of elongated toes

Arm used for moving and catching food

Fossil brittle star, *Palaeocoma*

Still here today

This 180-million-year-old fossil brittle star looks like the living relative above, which has five jointed arms that can easily break. It is often found on sandy or muddy sea beds.

Ancient coral

Corals were well preserved in rocks because of their hard skeletons, such as this 400-million-year-old fossil coral. The skeleton of each tiny coral animal joined that of its neighbour to create chains with spaces between them.

Changing oceans

A giant ocean, Panthalassa, surrounded the super-continent Pangaea (1), 290–240 mya (million years ago). At the end of this period, many kinds of marine life became extinct. Pangaea split apart, around the Tethys Sea.

Continental drift

The North Atlantic formed 208–146 mya (2). The South Atlantic and Indian oceans began to form 146–65 mya (3). The continents continued to drift 1.64 mya (4), and the oceans are still changing shape today.

Most flexible vertebrae in neck

Plated arm in life had feather-like feeding structures

Long neck and small head typical of one type of plesiosaur

Sharp, interlocking teeth for capturing fish prey

Marine reptiles

Early reptiles mostly lived on land, but some of their descendants adapted to life in the sea. Plesiosaurs first appeared around 200 million years go. They swam using their flippers as oars or wings to "fly" through water like turtles do today. They died out around 65 million years ago, as did their land-based cousins, the dinosaurs. The only marine reptiles today are the sea snakes and sea turtles.

Smaller, front flipper also had five elongated toes

All-round vision provided by large, curved eye

Sea lily

A whole fossil of a sea lily (crinoid) is quite rare. Large numbers of these animals grew on the bottom of ancient oceans, but the skeleton of small bony plates usually broke up when the animal died. Far less numerous now, sea lilies are still found living below 100 m (330 ft), usually anchored to the sea bed. Arms around their mouth trap small particles of food drifting by.

Long, flexible stem anchored crinoid in sea-bed gardens

Segmented body allowed trilobite to roll up like a woodlouse

Dead and gone

Once one of the most abundant creatures in ancient seas, trilobites flourished 510–250 million years ago. They had jointed limbs and an external skeleton like insects and crustaceans (such as crabs and lobsters).

Oceans today

Leafy sea dragon

All of Earth's sea water is linked in one continuous mass. The largest expanses are called oceans. Smaller ones (usually close to, or partly enclosed by, land) are called seas. Two-thirds of Earth's surface is covered by seawater, which makes up to 97 per cent of the planet's entire water supply. The temperature of seawater is colder at the surface in polar regions than in the tropics, and generally gets colder with depth. Salinity varies, too, as does the ocean floor – ranging from undersea mountains to plateaus, plains, and trenches.

Haiti/Dominican Republic

Sea level

Tobago

Trinidad

North coast of Venezuela

South America

Georgetown (capital of Guyana)

Continental shelf

Model (right) of a section of the sea floor east of the Caribbean, as shown in red square on map (below)

Guiana Plateau

Continental slope

Bering Sea

Arctic Ocean

Pacific Ocean

Sargasso Sea

Baltic Sea

Arabian Sea

Mediterranean Sea

Indian Ocean

Coral Sea

Tasman Sea

Southern Ocean

Caribbean Sea

Atlantic Ocean

Five oceans

The world's five oceans, from largest to smallest, are the Pacific, Atlantic, Indian, Southern, and Arctic. The Pacific covers 153 million sq km (62 million sq miles) and is about 13 times the size of the Arctic. The Arctic Ocean's centre is permanently covered by a layer of sea ice which expands in winter and shrinks in summer due to melting. Over half the Southern Ocean is also frozen in winter. The average depth of all the oceans is 3,650 m (12,000 ft).

Sea or lake?
Surrounded by desert, the Dead Sea is saltier than any ocean because the water that drains into it evaporates in the hot Sun; the body can float on the salts left behind. The Dead Sea is a lake, not a true sea, as it has no channel linking it to the ocean.

loating on the Dead Sea

God of the waters
Neptune, the Roman god of the sea, is often shown riding a dolphin and carrying a three-pronged spear (trident). He was also thought to control freshwater supplies.

Disappearing act
The gigantic tectonic plates on Earth's crust move like a conveyor belt. New areas of ocean floor form at spreading centres, and old areas sink below trenches where one oceanic plate is forced under another (subduction).

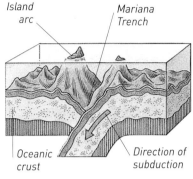

Island arc   *Mariana Trench*

Oceanic crust   *Direction of subduction*

Formation of Mariana Trench

Hatteras Abyssal Plain

Puerto Rico Trench

Nares Abyssal Plain

Mid-Atlantic Ridge

Kane Fracture Zone

Vema Fracture Zone

The ocean floor
This model shows the Atlantic Ocean off northeast South America. Off this coast is the continental shelf, under relatively shallow water about 200 m (660 ft) deep. The shelf is about 200 km (125 miles) wide here, but it is up to 1,600 km (1,000 miles) wide off northern Asia. From there, the ocean floor drops steeply, to form the continental slope. Sediments eroded from the land and carried by rivers accumulate at the bottom of this slope. The ocean floor then opens out in virtually flat abyssal plains. Deep trenches, such as the Puerto Rican Trench, can form where one of Earth's tectonic plates slides past another. An arc of volcanic islands has also been created where the North American Plate is forced under the Caribbean Plate.

Demerara Abyssal Plain

Ocean life

Oceans are home to some of the most diverse life on Earth. Animals live either on the sea bed or in mid-water where they swim or float. Plants are only found in the sunlit zone where there is enough light for them to grow, and are anchored to the sea floor or drifting in the water. Animals are found at all depths, but are most abundant in the sunlit zone where food is plentiful. Some animals move from one zone to another, to surface for air or to find more food. Over 90 per cent of all species dwell on the sea floor. One rock can house at least 10 major groups, such as corals and sponges.

Bloody Henry starfish

Common sunstar

Shore life
Often found on the shore at low tide, starfish also live in deeper water. Sea life on the shore must either be tough enough to withstand drying out, or shelter in rock pools.

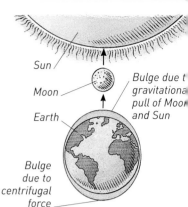

Sun

Moon

Earth

Bulge due t gravitationa pull of Moor and Sun

Bulge due to centrifugal force

Time and tide
Tides are caused by th gravitational pull of the Moon o Earth's sea water on one side c the planet and by centrifuga force on the opposite side As Earth spins around ove 24 hours, the bulges (high tides usually occur twice a day in an one place. The highest an lowest tides (spring tides) occu when the Moon and Sun are i line, causing the greates gravitational pul

Speedy squic
One of the most commor animals in the sea, squi often swim in shoals fo protection. Built lik streamlined torpedoes they can swim quickly

Inside squid's soft body is a horny, pen-like shell

Funnel expels jet of water for moving in sea

Tentacles reach out to grasp food

Note: Neither the marine life nor zones are drawn to scale

Deep-sea cat shark grows to only 50 cm (20 in) long

Continental shelf

Flying fish

Man-of-war

Shark

Oarweed

Mackerel

Turtle

Brain coral

Continental slope

Sperm whale

Sponges

Octopus

Hatchet fish

Sea pens

Rat-tail fishes

Gulper eel

Sea spider

Anglerfish

Sea cucumbers

Abyssal plain

Flower-basket sponge

Brittle star

Tripod fish

Deep-sea anemone

Sunlit zone
0–200 m
(0–660 ft)

Twilight zone
200–1,000 m
(660–3,300 ft)

Dark zone
1,000–4,000 m
(3,300–13,200 ft)

Abyss
4,000–6,000 m
(13,200–19,800 ft)

Trench
Over 6,000 m
(19,800 ft)

The ocean's zones
The ocean is divided into zones. In the sunlit zone, there is plenty of light, much water movement, and seasonal change in temperature. Beneath this is the twilight zone, where there is little light and temperatures drop rapidly with depth to about 5°C (41°F). Deeper yet is the dark zone, where there is no light and temperatures drop to about 1–2°C (34–36°F). Even deeper is the abyss and then the trenches. There are also zones on the sea bed, from the continental shelf to continental slope, abyssal plains, and trenches.

Giant among sea firs

Standing about 1 m (3.3 ft) tall on the sea bed, this giant sea fir was first discovered in 1875, when HMS *Challenger* scooped up a specimen off the coast of Japan. In 1985, living specimens were first observed from a submersible craft. The sea fir catches food drifting by in its long tentacles and can even tackle tiny fishes, up to 2 cm (1 in) long. It is found in the Pacific Ocean at 50–5,300 m (165–17,500 ft), and in the Atlantic Ocean.

Stinging tentacles surround mouth

Floating fronds can grow to 45 m (150 ft) long, forming a floating canopy on water's surface

Magnificent weed

Growing up from the sea bed, the giant kelp has a central, stem-like stalk, covered with leaf-like blades. Each blade has a gas-filled air bladder, which keeps the kelp afloat. Spreading out its blades, the kelp absorbs sunshine for making food by photosynthesis. Giant kelps grow over 0.3 m (1 ft) a day. Off North America's Pacific coast, kelp forests provide a home for fishes, sea otters, and sea urchins.

Long tentacles catch food drifting by in sea

Model of the largest known giant sea fir (*Branchiocerianthus imperator*)

First dorsal fin is placed well back on shark's body

Sea fir's stem grows out of muddy sand

Large pectoral fin

Deep-sea shark

Many people think of sharks as dangerous predators, but this cat shark from the deep Pacific Ocean is harmless. Some bony fishes have gas-filled air bladders to stop them sinking, but sharks have oil-rich livers instead.

Very long caudal (tail) fin

Icy ocean

There are two main types of sea ice: pack ice on the open sea (right) and fast ice between land and pack ice. Being salty, seawater freezes at lower temperatures than freshwater. Since cold water sinks and is replaced by warm water, it takes a long time before the water is cold enough for ice to form. Icebergs are huge chunks broken off polar ice sheets and glaciers.

Waves and weather

Sea water is always moving. Winds drive the waves and major surface currents are driven by the prevailing winds. Surface and deep-water currents help to modify the world's climate by moving cold water from polar regions towards the tropics, and vice versa. Heat from the oceans creates air movement. The ocean heats up more slowly than the land by day. Cool air above the water blows in, replacing warm air above the land, and the reverse at night.

Down the spou
Water spouts suck water u
when whirling air drops dow
from a storm cloud to the sea

Rivers of the sea

Currents are huge masses of water moving through the oceans. The course that currents follow is not precisely the same as the trade winds and westerlies, because currents are deflected by land and the Coriolis Force produced by Earth's rotation. The latter causes currents to shift to the right in the northern hemisphere and to the left in the southern.

North Pacifi Current

Peru Current

Brazil Current

Gulf Stream

West Wind Drift

South Equatoria Current

Day 2: Thunderstorms as swirling cloud mass

Day 4: Winds have increased in intensity

Day 7: Strong winds

A hurricane is born
These satellite images show a hurricane forming, from a swirling cloud mass to ferocious winds over seven days.

Ice forms at the very top of clouds

Hurricanes ar enormous – some may be 800 km (500 miles) across

Warm, moist air spirals up around eye inside hurricane

Torrential rains fall from clouds

Energy to driv storm comes from a warm ocean at 27°C (80°F) or more

Strongest winds of up to 360 kph (220 mph) occur just outside the eye

Hurricane!
Also known as typhoons hurricanes form in the tropics where warm, moist air rises up from the ocean's surface, creating storm clouds. As more air spirals upwards, the energy released fuels stronger winds that whirl around the eye (a calm area of extreme low pressure). Hurricanes cause devastation over land. Away from the ocean, they die out

Monitoring buoy

This buoy is moored to the sea bed and floats on the surface. Its instruments measure the winds and temperatures of the air and sea surface. The data is held in on-board computer systems and sent via satellite to a land-based station. Each buoy's location can be found by the signals it sends back to the satellite.

Making waves

Waves are formed by wind on the surface of the water, which causes friction. The wave moves forwards in the same direction as the wind, but the water making up the wave barely shifts at all. It follows a circular path, shown by the floating bottle (above). Waves driven towards a beach break when the water becomes too shallow.

Flashing light can be seen by ships

Antenna for transmitting satellite signals

Distance wave travels

Trough   _Crest_

Floating bottle

Wave moves on

Wave passes

Bottle has only moved a short distance

Propeller wind vane measures speed and direction of wind

Sensor measures air temperature

...ne to orient ...oy into wind

Tower measures 3 m (10 ft) high

Hull of buoy is 3 m (10 ft) across, big enough for a person to board it

Sensor measures temperature of sea's surface

...attered shore

...e highest waves (from ...ugh to crest) are driven ...high winds blowing across ...e ocean for long distances ...interrupted by land. ...e southwest coast ...England gets ...me of the biggest ...rm waves ...cause they come ...ht across the ...lantic Ocean.

...uoy for ...onitoring ...ean winds ...d temperatures

MET TEAM
IOSDL

Sandy and muddy

In shallow coastal waters, sand and mud are washed from the land to the edge of the continental shelf. Vast stretches of the sea floor look like underwater deserts. Finer-grained mud settles in places where the water is calmer. Without rocks, there are fewer seaweeds to provide shelter, so animals that venture onto the surface are exposed to predators. Many of these creatures avoid them by hiding in the soft sea bed. All the animals shown here live in the coastal waters of the Atlantic Ocean.

Tough papery tube protects soft worm inside

Worm can grow up to 40 cm (16 in) long

Bulky body 10 cm (4 in) long is covered by dense mat of fine hairs

Coarse, shiny bristles help it to move along sea bed

Bristling beauty

The sea mouse ploughs through muddy sand on the sea bed, eating any dead animals it finds. The rainbow-coloured spines help propel this chunky worm and may deter hungry fish. Keeping its rear end out of the sand brings in fresh sea water to help it breathe.

Thick trunk looks like a peanut, when whole body retracts

Light colour helps it merge into sand

Surface of plump, unsegmented body feels rough

Poisonous spines on first dorsal fin

Peanut worm

Many groups of worms live in the sea. This is one of 320 types of sipunculid – or peanut worms – which hide in the sand or in empty sea shells. A stretchy front part can retract into the thicker trunk.

Front part can also retract

Poisonous spine on front of gill cover

High-set eye allows all-round vision

Mouth surrounded by tentacles

Wary weever

When a weever fish is buried in sand, the eyes on top of its head help it see what is going on. Poisonous spines provide extra defence and can inflict nasty wounds if a weaver is trodden on or caught in a fishing net.

Flat fish

Flounders cruise along the sea bed looking for food. They nibble the tops off peacock worms.

Fan-shaped flaps beat to let food pass along worm's body

Parapodia, or feet-like flaps

Red seaweed grows on whitish ends of tube

Feeler-like palps (sense organs)

Tentacles fringed with fine hairs

Parapodia

Mouth

Parchment worm outside its tube

Fan-shaped flap

A look inside

The parchment worm lives in a U-shaped tube with ends that stick out above the mud's surface. It draws water containing food into its tube. Fan-shaped flaps waft the water along. Food is trapped in a slimy net that is rolled up and passed towards the mouth. A new net is then made and the process repeated.

When buried, the tube is often U-shaped

Parapodia

Parapodia

Tentacles disappear fast into tube, if danger is present

Like a peacock's fan

A crown of tentacles helps peacock worms feed and breathe. As water passes through the tentacles, particles in the water are passed down rows of tiny beating hairs into the mouth in the crown's centre. Larger particles help make the tube.

Peacock worm can be 25 cm (10 in) long

Tube made of mud and sand particles bound together with worm's hardened slime

Soft sea bed

On a soft sea bed, few animals are visible because most of them live buried in the sand. You may spot a crab's feathery antennae or a clam's siphon, which help these animals get a clean supply of oxygenated water to breathe. Some fish visit the soft sea bed to feed on burrowing clams. Other animals are found among sea grasses. These flowering plants are food for many animals.

Tough skin protects dugong

Docile dugong
Found in shallow tropical waters, this shy, gentle mammal feeds on sea grasses growing in the soft sea bed and digs out their roots.

Shell boat
In Botticelli's *The Birth of Venus*, the Roman goddess rises from the sea in a huge scallop shell. The real shell would fit in your hand.

Anemone-like polyp unfurls when feeding

Elegant pen
Shaped like a writing quill, this sea pen lives in the soft sea bed. Rows of tiny polyps unfurl on each side of its body to capture small animals drifting by. Sea pens glow in the dark if they are disturbed.

This sea pen can grow to 20 cm (8 in) in height

Long dorsal fin runs along almost whole length of body

Red band fish
This fish usually lives in burrows in the soft sea bed, as far down as 200 m (660 ft). It is also found swimming among sea grasses. When out of its burrow, the fish swims by passing waves down its body. It feeds on small animals.

Long anal fin

Red band fish may grow to 70 cm (28 in) in length

Stem of sea pen anchors in sandy sea bed

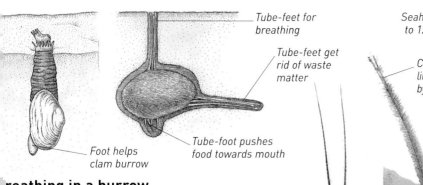

Tube-feet for breathing

Tube-feet get rid of waste matter

Foot helps clam burrow

Tube-foot pushes food towards mouth

Seahorse can be up to 12 cm (5 in) long

Crab's antennae linked together by bristles

Dorsal fin beats 20 to 35 times per second

Horse-like head

reathing in a burrow

he sand gaper clam (above left) pokes
vo tube-like siphons above the sand to
ter water in and out, for food particles
nd oxygen. A spiny sea urchin called
e sea potato (above right) uses its
be feet instead.

Front claw, or pincers

Seahorse uncurls tail to rise up in water

Masked crab

By day, this crab hides in the sand,
with only its two antennae sticking out.
These feelers link to form a breathing
tube when the crab is buried. Water
passes down the tube and over the
crab's gills. At night, the crab comes
out to find food such as small shrimp.

Handy tail

Seahorses are
usually found
among corals,
sea grasses, or
seaweeds. Unlike
most fish, they
swim with their
bodies upright and
move by waves
passing down their
dorsal fin. They feed on
small animals, sucking
them into their mouths.

Tail curls around seaweed

Face-like markings on shell give crab its name

Large eye helps to spot prey

Back leg used for digging

Eagle ray can grow to 200 cm (80 in) long

A "flying" ray

The eagle ray flaps its two
large, wing-like pectoral
fins as it swims along the
sea bed. It searches out
shellfish with its snout and
crushes them between
bands of flattened teeth.

Short pectoral fin

Pectoral fin, or wing

Bulgy, fleshy head

ointed nout

Rocks underwater

Rocks make up the sea bed in coastal waters, where currents sweep away any sand and mud. Animals must cling onto rocks, find crevices to hide in, or shelter in seaweeds. Piddocks (clams) and some sea urchins can bore into solid rock to make their homes. Some other animals hide under small stones lodged in the soft sea bed, but where masses of loose pebbles roll around, animals and seaweeds can be crushed. Some animals can survive at the water's edge, especially in rock pools, but many need to stay submerged.

Sea urchin boring into rocks

Piddock

Rock borers

Some sea urchins use their spines and teeth to bore holes in rock. Using its muscular foot, the piddock twists and turns to drill with the tip of its shell and hold onto its burrow.

Dorsal fin has eyespot to frighten predators

Beautiful butterfly

Blennies, small fishes living in shallow water, often rest on the sea floor and hide in small spaces. They lay their eggs in sheltered places, such as old bottles, and guard them from predators.

Spiny shell helps deter predators

Spiny lobster

European spiny lobsters have small pincers and are restricted to eating soft prey such as worms, or devouring dead animals. They live among rocks, hiding in crevices by day, but venture out over the sea bed to find food at night.

Delicate claw on tip of walking leg

European spiny lobster, also known as a crayfish or crawfish

Leg used for walking

Tail can be flapped so lobster can swim backwards

Monster claws

The savage sea monster in this old engraving looks like a lobster with two giant-sized pincers. Real lobsters can grow to 90 cm (35 in) long and weigh up to 20 kg (44 lb).

Very long antenna, or feeler

Compact crustacean

Squat lobsters can hide under stones, emerging at night in search of food. When threatened, they can swim a short distance by flapping their abdomen.

Small pincer to tear food

Body length up to 13 cm (5 in)

Abdomen tucks under body

Long dorsal fin

Each arm has rows of suckered tube-feet underneath

Mouth in centre of star, beneath the body

Diameter can be as much as 30 cm (12 in)

Rock star

Most starfish have five arms (or multiples of five). This purple sunstar, however, which is sometimes yellow or red, has 7–13 arms.

Fine feathers

Feather stars are echinoderms (creatures with body parts radiating from the centre), as are starfish, sea urchins, and sea lilies. Like most echinoderms, their body pattern is arranged in sets of five. This feather star uses 10 feathery arms to capture food particles in the water, crawl along the sea bed, swim, and hang onto rocks.

Tube-feet line the fine branches of the feathered arms

Arms span body and vary in size from 7–15 cm (3–6 in) long

19

On the rocks

In shallow, cool waters above rocky sea beds, forests of kelp (large brown seaweeds) are home to many sea creatures. Fish swim among the giant fronds. Sea otters wrap themselves in kelp while sleeping on the surface. Tightly gripping the rocks, the kelp's root-like anchor (holdfast) houses hordes of tiny creatures, such as worms and mites. Anchored to rocks, mussels provide homes for some animals between or within their shells.

A type of brown seaweed (kelp) from the Pacific Ocean

Marine mammal
Sea otters swim and rest among giant kelp fronds along North America's Pacific coast. They smash shellfish open on a rock balanced on their chest.

Anchored algae
Holdfasts of the large, tough, brown algae called kelp keep it firmly anchored to the rocks.

Hold on tight
Lumpsuckers cling to rocks with suckerlike fins on their bellies. They come into shallow water to breed and the father guards the eggs.

Scaleless body is covered with small, warty bumps

Juvenile lumpsucker

Each sturdy blunt finger measures at least 3 cm (1 in) across

Fleshy fingers supported by many, tiny, hard splinters

White, anemone-like polyp captures food from fast currents

Holdfast of oarweed kelp

Dead man's fingers
Growing on rocks, the colonies of this soft coral consist of many polyps (feeding bodies) within a fleshy, orange or white base.

Gills

Holdfast must be strong, as some kinds of kelp can grow tens of metres long

Microscopic sea mat
The lacy-looking growth on the kelp's surface (left) is a colony of bryozoans, or moss animals. Each little compartment houses one of these animals, which come out to capture food in their tiny tentacles. Other kinds of moss animal grow upwards, looking like seaweeds or corals. Between the sea mats, a blue-rayed limpet grazes on the kelp's surface.

Sea slug
Many sea slugs are meat eaters. This slug lives on the soft coral known as dead man's fingers. Sea slug eggs hatch into swimming young, which then settle and turn into adults.

Long legs

The long-legged, aptly-named spider crab hides under rocks and among seaweeds on the lower shore and in shallow waters, hanging on with its claws. To blend in, it plucks bits of seaweed with its pincers and attaches them to its shell.

Pea crab may nibble mussel's gills

Horse mussel and friends

Heavy-shelled horse mussels live in colonies on rocks or kelp holdfasts in shallow water, attached by tough threads. Tiny creatures live among the mussels, but the pea crab lives within the shell, feeding on the mussel's food.

Seaweeds growing on mussel shell

Seaweed on legs as part camouflage

Sharp-tipped claw for hanging onto seaweed

Horse mussel grows to 20 cm (8 in) long

Feathery tentacles held on tough, single stems

Anemone-like polyp with two rings of tentacles to capture food

Sea mat growing on surface

ea flowers

his sea fir (hydroid) looks
bit like a flowering plant,
ut it belongs to the same
roup of animals as corals,
llyfish, and sea anemonies.
ea firs grow fixed to surfaces,
uch as rocks and seaweeds,
ith branching out colonies of
nemone-like polyps. These have
entacles that are used to capture
ood particles carried past in the
urrent. If disturbed, the sea fir
ill withdraw its polyps into its
orny skeleton.

The coral kingdom

In the clear, warm waters of the tropics, coral reefs cover vast areas. Most stony corals are colonies of many tiny, anemone-like polyps. Each polyp makes a hard limestone cup (skeleton) that protects its soft body. They do this with the help of microscopic, single-celled algae that live inside them. The algae need sunlight to grow, so coral reefs are found only in sunny, surface waters. Only the upper layer of a reef is made of living corals, which build upon skeletons of dead polyps. It is also home to soft corals and sea fans, which do not have stony skeletons.

Tentacle's stings catch food

Hard plates of stony skeleton

Mouth expels waste

Bag-lik stomac

Inside a coral animal
Polyps are linked by a layer of tissue. To reproduce, they divide in two or release eggs and sperm.

Black coral's horny skeleton looks like a bunch of twigs

Orange sea fan from the Indian and Pacific Oceans

Stinging coral
Colourful hydrocorals are related to sea firs. Known as fire corals, they have potent stings on their polyps.

Black coral
In living black corals, the skeleton provides support for the living tissues and the branches bear rows of anemone-like polyps. Mainly tropical, it grows in the deep part of coral reefs.

Intricate mesh developed to withstand strong currents

Stem of sea fan

Sea fan

Sea fans are gorgonian corals that have soft tissues growing around a central horny or chalky skeleton. They are more closely related to sea pens, organ-pipe coral, and soft corals than to true stony corals. Most kinds live in tropical waters. Some sea fans form branching, tree-like shapes (left), but in others the branches join together to form a broad, fan-shaped network.

Fringing reef grows around volcano

As volcano subsides, lagoon appears, creating barrier reef

Volcano disappears, leaving behind coral atoll

Atoll in the making

An atoll is a ring of coral islands around a central lagoon. Charles Darwin (1809–82) realized they grew around a volcanic island, which then sank.

Brittle skeleton of organ-pipe coral breaks easily

Queen scallops living within the rose coral's folds

Branching tree-like skeleton

Living rose coral (not a true coral) can reach 50 cm (20 in) in diameter

ral's convoluted e looks like that f a human brain

Organ pipes

In the living organ-pipe coral, anemone-like polyps emerge from the bright red skeleton's tiny pipes. This is not a true stony coral, but a relative of sea fans, soft coral, and sea pens.

A coral by any other name

Rose coral is a moss animal, growing on the sea bed in colonies made of millions of tiny animals.

Biggest and best

More than 2,000 km (1,200 miles) long, Australia's Great Barrier Reef is the largest structure in the world made by living organisms. It includes 400 kinds of coral.

Stone brain

The surface of living brain coral is covered with soft issue. Anemone-like polyps grow in rows along the hannels in this slow-growing, stony coral's skeleton.

Life on a coral reef

Mantle

A giant clam

The giant blue clam grows to about 30 cm (12 in) long. A horde of single-celled algae in its brightly coloured mantle uses energy from sunlight to make their own food. The clam absorbs nutrients from the algae.

Coral reefs support an amazing variety of marine life. Every bit of space provides shelter for some animal or plant. At night, a host of creatures emerges from coral caves and crevices to feed. All these living organisms depend on the stony corals that recycle scarce nutrients from the clear, blue, tropical waters. People, as well as animals, rely on coral reefs as they protect coastlines, and some island nations live on coral atolls. Sadly, coral reefs are under threat, damaged by snorkellers and divers treading on them, dynamited by fishermen, and polluted by sewage and oil spills.

Green colour helps camouflage sea slug amongst seaweed

Tentacles of sea anemone covered with stings to put off predators

The clown fish's slimy coat does not trigger the anemone's stings

Large eye for keeping a watch for danger

Frilly lettuce

Sea slugs are related to sea snails but do not have shells. Many feed on the coral but the lettuce slug feeds on algae growing on the reef, by sucking the sap from their cells. Stored in the slug's digestive system, chloroplasts, the green part of plant cells, continue to trap energy from sunlight to make food.

Side fin used to steer and change direction

Stripes break up clown fish's outline, making it more difficult for predators to see the fish on the reef

Living in harmony

Clown fish shelter in anemones living on coral reefs in the Pacific and Indian oceans. Unlike other fish, clown fish do not trigger the stings of their anemone home, because chemicals taken from the anemone are carried in the clown fish's slimy coat. Certain kinds of clown fish live only with certain kinds of anemones.

Date mussel

This date mussel makes its home by producing chemicals to wear a hole in the hard coral. It filters food particles from water passing through its gills.

Date mussel on a coral reef in the Red Sea

Narrow snout probes rocks for sponges and other animals

Colours help attract mate

Plain yellow caudal (tail) fin

Adult

Adult's colours and patterns act as signals to other angelfish

Growing up

The young emperor angelfish looks different from the adult, and its colours may protect it better. Once adults pair up and establish territories on the reef, their colours and patterns help other emperors to recognize them and keep off their patch.

Juvenile

Ring patterns may draw predator away from juvenile's more vulnerable head

Glands in skin make slug taste bad to deter predators

Flat, slimy foot under the frilly body

Soft body has no shell to protect slug

Green colour shows slug eats algae

Notorious starfish

The crown-of-thorns starfish eats the soft parts of a gorgonian coral. Like many other starfish, it turns its stomach inside out, making enzymes to digest its prey. Plagues of these starfish can wreck a reef.

Crown-of-thorns starfish eating coral

Tentacles can be pulled back inside body for protection

Tentacles around mouth used for feeding

Tough skin

Lettuce slug breathes through its leafy-looking skin

One of five rows of tube-feet that help sea cucumber to crawl

Colourful cucumber

This colourful sea cucumber lives on or close to reefs in the Indo-Pacific region. Sea cucumbers are echinoderms (p. 19), like starfish, sea urchins, and sea lilies. Sea cucumbers put out sticky tentacles to catch small particles of food and put them in their mouth.

Special fat tentacles for smelling food

Sea meadows

The most abundant plants in the ocean are minute floating plants called phytoplankton. Like all plants they need sunlight to grow, and live in the ocean's upper zone. Light is most abundant in the tropics but nutrients are in short supply here. Huge phytoplankton blooms are found in cooler waters where nutrients (dead plant and animal waste) are brought up from the bottom during storms, and in both cool and warm waters where there are upwellings of nutrient-rich water. Phytoplankton are mostly eaten by tiny animals (zooplankton), which are eaten by small fish, which in turn are eaten by larger predators; some of the biggest fish and whales feed directly on zooplankton.

Plant food
This diatom is one of many phytoplankton that drift in the ocean. Many diatoms are single cells, but this one consists of a chain of cells.

Glass jar to collect plankton sample

Plankton enters net at wide end

Older stage crab larva showing pincers

In the net
Scientists use special nets to study plankton. Commercial fishing relies on how much plankton there is for young fish to eat. Phytoplankton also help regulate our climate because they use so much carbon dioxide – one of the gases responsible for global warming.

Very fine mesh net traps tiny plants and animals drifting in the ocean

Younger stage crab larva

Ocean in bloom
Two images from a space satellite show phytoplankton densities in the Atlantic Ocean. Red shows where phytoplankton is densest through yellow, green, blue to violet where it is least dense. Phytoplankton's spring bloom (right) occurs when days are longer and more nutrients come up from the bottom. A second, smaller bloom of phytoplankton occurs in the autumn.

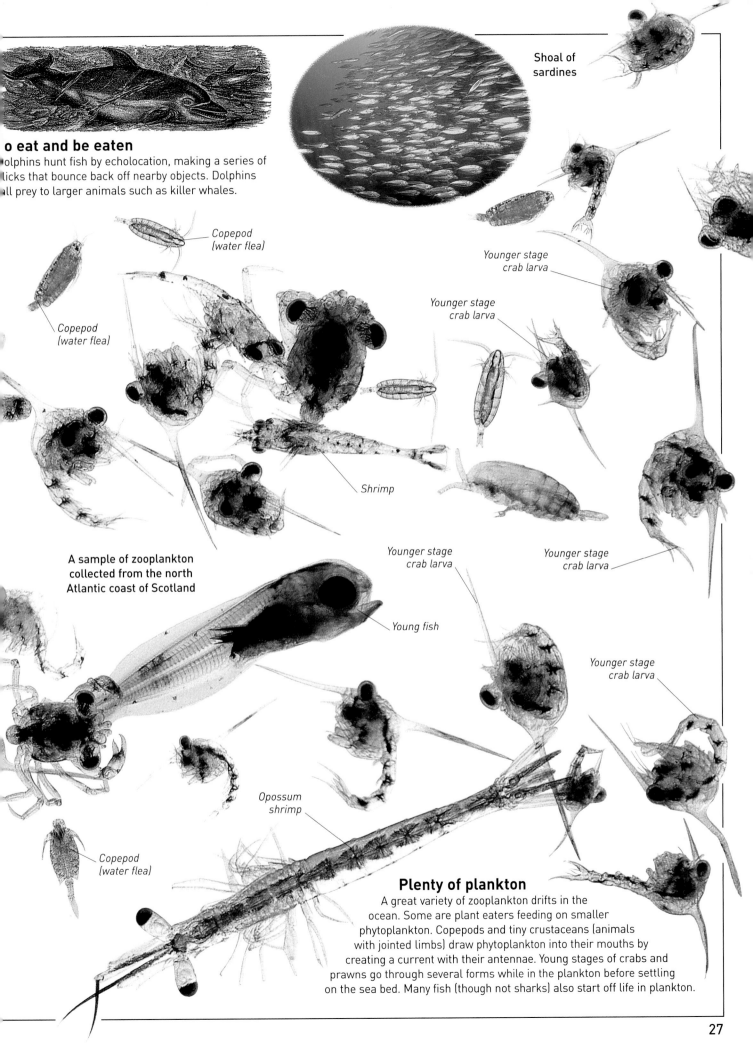

o eat and be eaten

olphins hunt fish by echolocation, making a series of
licks that bounce back off nearby objects. Dolphins
ll prey to larger animals such as killer whales.

Shoal of
sardines

*Copepod
(water flea)*

*Copepod
(water flea)*

*Younger stage
crab larva*

*Younger stage
crab larva*

Shrimp

**A sample of zooplankton
collected from the north
Atlantic coast of Scotland**

*Younger stage
crab larva*

*Younger stage
crab larva*

Young fish

*Younger stage
crab larva*

*Opossum
shrimp*

*Copepod
(water flea)*

Plenty of plankton

A great variety of zooplankton drifts in the
ocean. Some are plant eaters feeding on smaller
phytoplankton. Copepods and tiny crustaceans (animals
with jointed limbs) draw phytoplankton into their mouths by
creating a current with their antennae. Young stages of crabs and
prawns go through several forms while in the plankton before settling
on the sea bed. Many fish (though not sharks) also start off life in plankton.

Predators

Some ocean animals are herbivores (plant eaters), which feed on seaweeds or phytoplankton.

There are also many carnivores (meat eaters), large and small. Some are swift hunters; others set traps for their prey, waiting to attack with snapping jaws or stinging tentacles. Many animals strain food out of the water, and seabirds dive for a beakful of prey Omnivores eat both plants and animals.

Co-operative feedin

Humpback whales encircle a shoal of fis gulp in water and food, then expel th water through sieve like baleen plate in their mouth

Caught by slime

Many jellyfish sting their prey, but the common jellyfish traps tiny plankton in mucus from its bell. Four arms collect up the food-laden slime and tiny hair-like cilia channel it into the mouth.

Tiny prey caught in mucus

Fang face

The wolf fish has strong, fang-like teeth that crunch through the hard shells of crabs, sea urchins, and mussels. As the front set is worn down each year, or broken, it is replaced by a new set growing behind.

Dorsal fin runs along entire length of body

Crooked, yellow fang-like teeth

Pectoral fin

Tough, wrinkled skin helps protect wolf fish living near the sea bed

pines to protect urchin

Grazing away

The European common sea urchin grazes on seaweeds and animals such as sea mats that grow on the surface of the seaweeds. It uses the rasping teeth on the underside of its shell. If too many sea urchins are collected for food or tourist souvenirs, a rocky reef can become overgrown by seaweed.

Sea urchin's mouth surrounded by five rasping teeth

Tube-feet used to walk slowly along the sea bed

Tiny teeth of a basking shark

Pelican diving

Pouch-like beak

Feeding on fishes

Like all pelicans, the brown pelican has a big beak with a large pouch of skin to capture fish. Only brown pelicans dive far below the surface for their prey. When the pelican surfaces, it drains the water from its pouch and swallows the fish.

To bite or not to bite

A tiger shark's pointed, serrated teeth can pierce and slice through almost anything, from hard-shelled turtles to seals and seabirds. A basking shark's rows of tiny teeth are not used at all – it filters food from water with a sieve of gill rakers.

Tiger shark's tooth

Any undigested pieces of food are ejected through the mouth

Stinging tentacle

Tentacle traps

Flower-like Dahlia anemones are deadly traps for prawns and small fish that brush past the tentacles. Hundreds of nematocysts (stinging cells) fire their stings, and the tentacles pass the stricken prey to the mouth in the centre – the entrance to the bag-like stomach.

Sucker-like disc lets Dahlia anemone attach to any hard surface

29

Homes and hiding

Staying hidden is one of the best means of defence – if a predator cannot see you, it is less likely to eat you! Many sea animals shelter among seaweeds, in rocky crevices, or under the sand. Camouflage matching the colours and the texture of the background also helps sea creatures remain undetected. The sargassum fish even looks like bits of seaweed. Hard shells give protection from weak-jawed predators. Sea snails and clams make their own shells that cover the body, while crabs and lobsters have outer shells, like suits of armour, covering the body and each jointed limb.

Blending in
Cuttlefish have different coloured pigments and rapidly change colour to escape predators. The brain signals tiny bags of pigment in its skin to contract, making the skin paler.

Cuttlefish becomes darker when pigment bags expand

What a weed
This fish lives among floating clumps of sargassum seaweed, where frilly growths on its head, body, and fins help it avoid being seen by predators, making a realistic disguise.

Hermit crab leaving old whelk shell

Anemone

Investigating its new home by checking size with its claws

When out of its shell, the crab is vulnerable to predators

Hermit crab moves into a perspex shell

All change
Hermit crabs lack armour around their abdomen, so they live in the empty shells of sea snails and other creatures. Like all crustaceans, a hermit crab grows by shedding its hard, outer skeleton and does this in the safety of its snail shell home. As it grows larger, it looks for a larger snail shell to move into. When it finds one that is just right, it carefully pulls its body out of its old shell, tucking it quickly into the new one.

Leg with pointed claws to get a grip on sea bed when walking

Antenna

Shells on shells

Carrier shells are sea snails that attach empty shells and bits of coral, stone, and broken glass to their own shells. This debris is a disguise against predators such as fish. It may also make it more difficult for fish to crack open the shell to reach the soft meat inside.

ours on
nderside
elp raise
hell off
ea bed

Tip of abdomen (the tail-end of the body) has an appendage to grip inner whorl of shell

Abdomen brought forward to shell opening to deposit droppings, so crab does not foul its shell

Pincer also used to pick up food

Another home

Some kinds of hermit crab do not move home, but extend their shell by placing a cloak anemone near its entrance. Others just place anemones on top of their shell, using their stings for protection, while the anemone picks up scraps of food from the crab.

Crab's soft body winds around shell's spirals

Home sweet home

The European hermit crab first makes its home in smaller shells, such as a periwinkle shell or topshell, which it finds on the shore. When the crab grows larger, it usually lives in whelk shells. Hermit crabs carry their homes around with them and the females rear the eggs inside their shells.

Large pincer, or cheliped, used to block entrance to shell, so providing extra security

Attack and defence

Many sea creatures have weapons to attack prey or defend themselves from predators. Some produce venom (poison) for defence and often warn of their danger with markings. The lionfish's stripes may alert enemies to its venomous spines, but being easy to see, they hunt at dusk when they can surprise their prey. Disappearing in a cloud of ink is a useful trick used by octopuses, squid, and cuttlefish. But no defence method is foolproof, as even the most venomous jellyfish can be eaten by carnivorous turtles that are immune to their stings.

Deadly stonefish
Never tread on a stonefish. Sharp spines on its back inject a venom that causes such pain that the shock can kill.

Ink cloud forming around cuttlefish

Long, dorsal spine with venom glands in grooves

Ink screen
Cephalopods (squid, cuttlefish, and octopuses) produce a cloud of ink to confuse an enemy and allow time to flee. The ink is ejected in a jet of water from a tube-like funnel near the head.

Horny projection above eye

Maerl (a chalky, red seaweed) grows in a thick mass along the stony sea bed

Three venomous anal spines

Blue for danger
If this octopus senses danger, blue-ringed spots appear on its skin, warning of its poisonous bite. Living in shallow, often tropical waters, this blue-ringed octopus is the size of your hand, but its bite can be fatal.

Keep clear
A predator trying to bite a stripey lionfish may be impaled by one or more of its poisonous spines. If it survives, the predator will remember the stripes and the danger and leave lionfish alone in future. Found in tropical waters, lionfish can swim openly looking for smaller prey with little risk of attack.

Stripes warn predators that lionfish is dangerous

Two venomous spines on tail can pierce the swimmer's skin and inject its venom

Sting ray's sting is sharp and serrated, easily piercing the skin

Pectoral fin used for swimming

Sting in the tail

This blue-spotted ray lives in warm waters and is often found lurking on the sandy sea bed. If trodden on, shooting pains occur in the foot for over an hour.

Something scary

Early sailors knew that some creatures of the deep were deadly. Tales about sea monsters were often greatly exaggerated. They were also made up to account for ships lost at sea.

Vicious jellyfish

Jellyfish are known for their stings, but the nastiest stings are those of the box jellyfish in the Pacific Ocean. They produce welts on anyone who comes in contact with their tentacles. A badly stung person can die in four minutes.

When shell is closed, there is still a gap between the shell's two halves

Tentacles always on show

Shaggy shells

These gaping file shells cannot pull their orange tentacles inside the two halves of their shell for protection, so the tentacles produce a sticky, sour-tasting substance to deter predators. Gaping file shells also put out byssus threads for anchorage. If dislodged, they can move by expelling water from their shell and using their tentacles like oars.

Shell is up to 2.5 cm (1 in) long

The jet set

One way to swim quickly and escape from predators is by jet propulsion. Some molluscs, such as clams, squid, and octopuses, do this by squirting water from the body cavity. Squid are best at this – their bodies are streamlined to reduce drag (resistance to water). Some kinds of scallops also use jet propulsion and are among the few clams that can swim. If attacked, the common octopus uses this same technique to jet off.

Tentacle tales
A Norwegian story tells of the Kraken, a sea monster that wrapped its giant arms around ships and sank them. The legend may be based on the mysterious giant squid that live in deep waters. Dead individuals have been found, but in 2004 a living one was finally photographed.

Jet propulsion
The engines powering a jet plane produce jets of air to fly. An octopus uses jets of water to dart through the sea.

Funnel

Long arms to grasp prey

Flexible funnel
At the edge of the octopus's bag-like body is a funnel. It can bend to aim the jet of water backwards or forwards.

Powerful suckers grip the rock, so octopus can pull itself along

1 On the bottom
The common octopus hides during the day in its rocky lair, coming out at night to look for such food as crustaceans.

Sucker i. sensitive to touch and tast

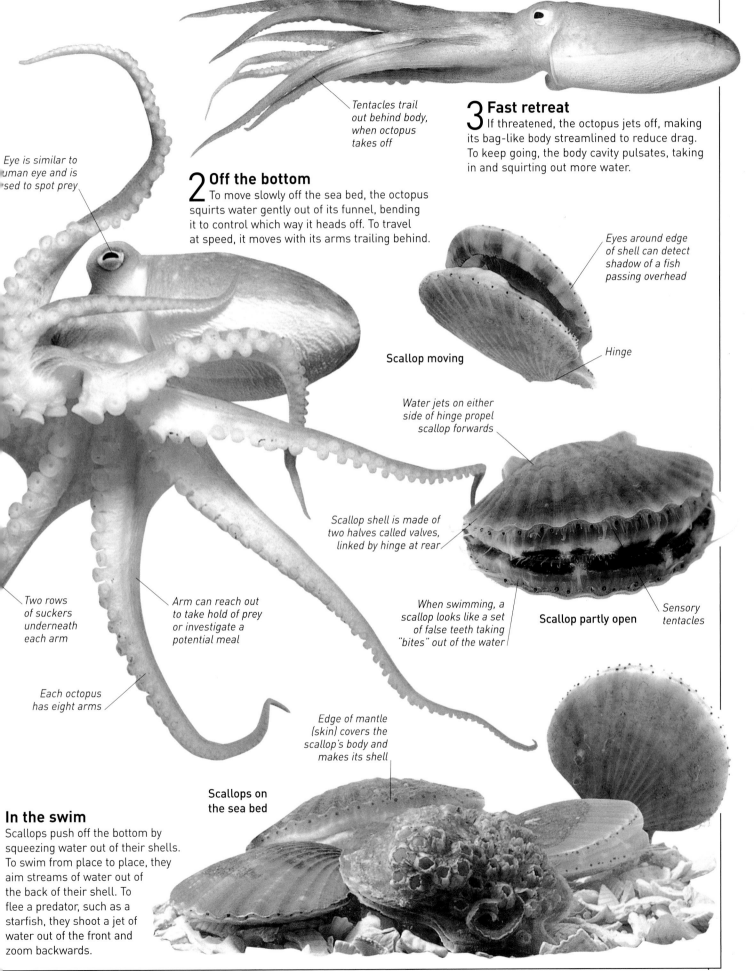

Tentacles trail out behind body, when octopus takes off

Eye is similar to human eye and is used to spot prey

2 Off the bottom
To move slowly off the sea bed, the octopus squirts water gently out of its funnel, bending it to control which way it heads off. To travel at speed, it moves with its arms trailing behind.

3 Fast retreat
If threatened, the octopus jets off, making its bag-like body streamlined to reduce drag. To keep going, the body cavity pulsates, taking in and squirting out more water.

Eyes around edge of shell can detect shadow of a fish passing overhead

Hinge

Scallop moving

Water jets on either side of hinge propel scallop forwards

Two rows of suckers underneath each arm

Arm can reach out to take hold of prey or investigate a potential meal

Scallop shell is made of two halves called valves, linked by hinge at rear

When swimming, a scallop looks like a set of false teeth taking "bites" out of the water

Scallop partly open

Sensory tentacles

Each octopus has eight arms

Edge of mantle (skin) covers the scallop's body and makes its shell

Scallops on the sea bed

In the swim
Scallops push off the bottom by squeezing water out of their shells. To swim from place to place, they aim streams of water out of the back of their shell. To flee a predator, such as a starfish, they shoot a jet of water out of the front and zoom backwards.

Moving along

Flying fish

Flying fish gather speed, leap into the air, and spread their side fins to glide for more than 30 seconds.

At school

Fish often swim together in a shoal or a school (like these blue-striped snappers). The moving mass of fish makes it harder for a predator to target one individual and there are more pairs of eyes to detect danger.

Seawater is much denser than air, making it harder to move through. To be a fast swimmer, it helps to have a shape that is streamlined like a torpedo to reduce drag (resistance to water). The density of seawater also helps to support an animal's body weight – the heaviest animal of all is the blue whale, which weighs up to 150 tonnes (165 US tons). Some ocean animals get up enough speed underwater to leap briefly into the air, but not all are good swimmers. Many can only swim slowly, or drift in the currents, crawl along the bottom, or burrow in the sand. Others simply stay put, anchored to the sea bed.

In the swing

During the day, many electric rays hide on the sandy bottom, relying on their electric organs for defence, but they swim if disturbed and at night in search of prey. There are about 20 members of the electric ray family, mostly living in warm waters. Most other rays have spindly tails (unlike the electric ray's broad tail), and move through water using their pectoral fins.

Electric ray's smooth skin can be either blackish or red-brown in colour

Water enters through spiracle and is pumped out through gill slits underneath

Some electric rays grow to 1.8 m (6 ft) and weigh up to 50 kg (110 lb)

Swimming sequence of an electric ray

Pelvic fin

Diving deep

True seals use front flippers to steer, and move by beating their back flippers and tail from side to side. Harbour seals (right) can dive to 90 m (300 ft), but the elephant seal dives to over 1,500 m (4,900 ft). When underwater, seals close their nostrils to stop water entering the airways, and use oxygen stored in the blood.

Broad tail fin, swinging from side to side, helps propel ray along

Pectoral fin provides extra propulsion as waves pass along flexible edges of its rounded side

Larger, first dorsal fin

Smaller, second dorsal fin

Clasper (male reproductive organ)

Eye

Electric organ, beneath skin at base of pectoral fin, helps catch fish by stunning them – some species produce over 200 volts

Dolphin's flipper

Flipper's flipper
The ancestors of whales and dolphins once lived on land. As they adapted to life in the sea, the four stocky limbs were modified into flippers and the hind limbs were eventually lost. The broad flipper of a dolphin is supported by five digits spread wide.

Scapula (shoulder blade)

Humerus (upper arm bone)

Ulna (lower arm bone)

Out of the water
Dolphins leap out of water to signal to other dolphins, when feeding, and for fun. They also porpoise (skim over water for short distances) when moving at speed.

Bottlenose dolphins can reach speeds of up to 27 kph (17 mph)

Phalange (toe bone)

Metacarpal (short, strong finger bone)

Buoyancy chamber

As nautilus grows, larger chambers form

Afloat
The gas-filled sections of the chambered nautilus's shell help to keep it afloat. The nautilus itself lives in the last and biggest chamber, and moves by jet propulsion (pp. 34–35).

Ocean travellers

Some sea animals travel great distances to find the best places to feed and breed. Whales feed in the cold, food-rich waters of the far north or south, then travel to the warm waters of the tropics to breed. Turtles, seals, and seabirds feed out at sea, but come ashore to reproduce. Salmon grow in the ocean and return to rivers to breed. Ocean currents help to speed animals on their way. Even animals that cannot swim can hitch a ride on another animal or drift on a piece of wood.

Back pair of flippers used as rudders to steer turtle along

Stalked barnacles on driftwood

Barnacles adrift

Barnacles grow on rocks, ships' hulls, and even turtles and whales. These goose barnacles can drift long distance on pieces of wood. Barnacles are crustaceans (like crabs and lobsters) and have shell-like plates that protect their bodies.

Broad surface of front flipper for ease of swimming

Larger eyes form when adult eel migrates to sea

Skin turns silver before eel migrates back to Sargasso Sea

Leaf-like larva (young), called Leptocephalus

Trailing tentacles armed with vicious stings

Young eel, known as elver or glass eel

Mysterious journey

For centuries, no one knew where European eels went to breed, only that young eels returned to rivers in large numbers. Then scientists found the smallest larvae were in the Sargasso Sea in the western Atlantic where the adult breed. The larvae drift back to Europe and turn into elvers.

Portuguese man-of-war

Not a true jellyfish but a siphonophore (a relative of sea firs), the man-of-war has a gas-filled float that keeps it at the surface where it is blown by the wind and drifts with the currents

Swimming sequence of a green turtle

Turtle shell is streamlined for gliding through water

nderwater flier

reen turtles live in warm waters in the Atlantic, Pacific, nd Indian oceans. Like all turtles, they come ashore to y their eggs. First the females mate in shallow ater with the waiting males. Later, at ght, the females crawl up the beach lay their eggs in the sand before eturning to the water. ome travel hundreds f kilometres to the each where they emselves atched out.

Front pair of flippers help turtle to "fly" through water

Turtles are air breathers, so must come to surface to breathe through their nostrils

Green turtle (*Chelonia mydas*) is endangered

Turtle trip

In Japanese legend, Urashima Taro rides into the sea on a turtle. After some time, he yearns for home. The sea goddess gives him a box that he must never open. Back home, he finds everything has changed and no one knows him. He opens the box and breaks the spell, turning into a very old man because he has spent 300 years at sea.

The twilight zone

Between the sunlit waters of the upper ocean and the black depths is the twilight zone, around 200–1,000 m (660–3,300 ft) below the surface. Fish living here often have rows of light organs on their bellies to help camouflage them against the little light that filters down from above. Many animals shelter in the twilight zone by day, hiding from daytime hunters such as seabirds, and then swim upwards to feed in the food-rich surface water at night. Others spend most of their lives here, eating any available food.

Hunter of the depths
Viper fish have an impressive set of long, dagger-like teeth to grab their fish prey, which they attract with a lure dangling from the front of the dorsal fin. To swallow prey, such as a hatchet fish (above left), the hinged jaws open very wide.

Fin ray

Jumbo squid can reach 3.6 m (12 ft) to tips of tentacles

Sail-like dorsal fin can be raised and lowered

A giant of a squid
The Atlantic giant squid can weigh as much as one tonne. Suckers on the tentacles cling onto prey, and sperm whales often bear the scars of an attack.

Dorsal fin can be used for herding fish prey

Mythical merman
Strange creatures lurk in the depths, but nothing like this.

Large gill flap

Model of a lancet fish

Pointed teeth for grabbing fish

Pectoral fin

Long and skinny
The lancet fish has a narrow body, lightweight bones, and little muscle. It catches squid and other fish living at the same depths.

Pelvic fin

Glass jellies

Glass jellyfish live in every ocean, from the sunlit upper zone to depths of 700 m (2,300 ft). They have a deep bell and a long mouth, which twists round to catch any prey. They can also display beautiful rainbow colours.

Sharply-angled dorsal fin

Model of a hatchet fish, Sternoptyx

Silvery body helps camouflage fish in right light

Large eye helps spot prey in the dark

Light organs also found under tail

Luminous patches in the mouth can attract prey right inside the jaw

Light organs located on belly

Deep-sea hatchet

Hatchet fish have silvery, blade-like bodies. The light organs along their belly and tail, when viewed from below, are just bright enough to help them blend in with the sunlit water above. Hatchet fish live in the Atlantic, Pacific, and Indian oceans.

Upward-pointing eye helps locate prey

Model of a hatchet fish, Opisthoproctus

Large, first dorsal fin

Symmetrical tail fin

Anus contains a colony of luminescent bacteria that generate light

Tube along belly produces light to avoid being spotted from below by predators

Looking up

There is more than one type of hatchet fish. This one has large, tubular eyes pointing upwards so it can detect the faintest glimmer of light produced by potential prey. This fish is found in oceans around the world below regions with warm surface waters.

Asymmetrical caudal (tail) fin

Extremely tiny second dorsal fin is fleshy

Lancet fish swims below the warm surface waters of the Atlantic, Pacific, and Caribbean

Colours (instead of light organs) help fish blend into light ocean above and dark ocean below

Lancet fish can grow nearly 2 m (6.5 ft) long

The darkest depths

There is no light in the oceans below 1,000 m (3,300 ft), just blackness. Many fish in the dark zone are black too and almost invisible. Light organs are used as signals to find a mate or to lure prey. Food is scarce in the cold, dark depths so most deep-sea animals are small. Fish with huge mouths and stretchy stomachs make the most of what little food rains down from above.

Lateral line organs sense vibrations in water made by moving prey

Umbrella mouth gulper

The gulper eel swims along slowly with its huge mouth wide open, ready to swallow any food it finds, such as shrimp and small fish. The adults live in the lower part of the twilight zone and in the dark zone. The leaf-like larvae are found in the sunlit zone from 100–200 m (330–660 ft). As they grow, the young gulper eels descend into deeper water.

Adults grow to about 75 cm (30 in) from the tip of their long tail to the head

Gulper eel lives in the dark depths below temperate and tropical surface waters

Long lower jaw

Tiny eye on end of nose

Fishing lin

The whipnose has a long, whip-like lu for attracting passing prey. The pr approaches, mistaking the lure fo food, and is then snapped u

Whipnose grows to 13 cm (5 in) in length

Monster movies

Films often feature scary sea monsters. So much of the deep ocean is unexplored that there could be strange animals yet to be discovered – they would most likely be small, as there is so little food at these depths.

Model of a whipnose, which lives in the Atlantic and Pacific oceans

Binocular eyes

Gigantura's extraordinary tubular eyes are probably used to pinpoint the glowing light organs of its prey. Its skin can stretch so that it can swallow fish larger than itself.

Lower lobe of tail fin is longer than upper lobe

Model of a *Melanocetus* anglerfish before a meal

Lure contains luminous bacteria used to attract prey and males

...oing fishing

...nglerfish are not just found in the ...eep. This one, from shallow waters, ...ses a worm-like lure ...n the end of its ...orsal fin ray ... attract prey ...assing by.

Model of anglerfish after a meal

Female of anglerfish can grow to 8 cm (3 in) long

Small eye typical of fish of the dark zone

Teeth bend backwards, allowing passage of large prey into mouth

Caudal fin

...eep-sea angler

...rey is guided towards ...he gaping jaws of the ...eep-sea angler by ... glow-in-the-dark lure. ...arge teeth, curving ...ackward, trap the prey ...nce it is within its jaws. ...he prey is swallowed ...hole. Male deep-sea ...nglers are up to 20 times ...maller than the females ...nd either feed on much ...maller prey, such as ...hrimp, or do not feed ...t all. Once a male finds ... female he hangs on by his ...aws. *Melanocetus* has been ...ound with a lantern fish twice ...ts own size in its stomach!

Big, stretchy stomach allows deep-sea anglerfish to take huge meals

Extraordinary eyes look like binoculars

Tough jelly

Atolla jellyfish are as tough as fruit gums. The reddish-brown colour is typical of deep-sea jellyfish. If disturbed, *Atolla* glows in the dark with a bluish light.

Model of *Gigantura*

On the bottom

The bottom of the deep ocean is not an easy place to live. There is little food, and it is dark and cold. Much of the sea bed is covered with soft clays or mud-like oozes made of skeletons of tiny sea animals and plants. Some animals feed on the sea bed, extracting small food particles from the ooze. While others filter nutrients from the water. These tiny food particles are the remains of dead animals (and their droppings) and plants that have sunk down from above. Because food is scarce and temperatures so low, most animals living in the deep ocean take a long time to grow.

Telegraph cables being laid along the bottom of the Atlantic Ocean, c. 1870

Dried remains of sea anemones

Glass-rope sponge
This cup-shaped sponge grows anchored to the soft sea bed by its long stem of glassy, needle-like strands. Sea anemones often grow on the stem.

Stem formed by long, glassy spikes made of silica

Not a true spider
Sea spiders belong to a group called pycnogonids. Some deep-sea spiders have a leg span of 60 cm (23.5 in) across, and can stride along without stirring up clouds of particles.

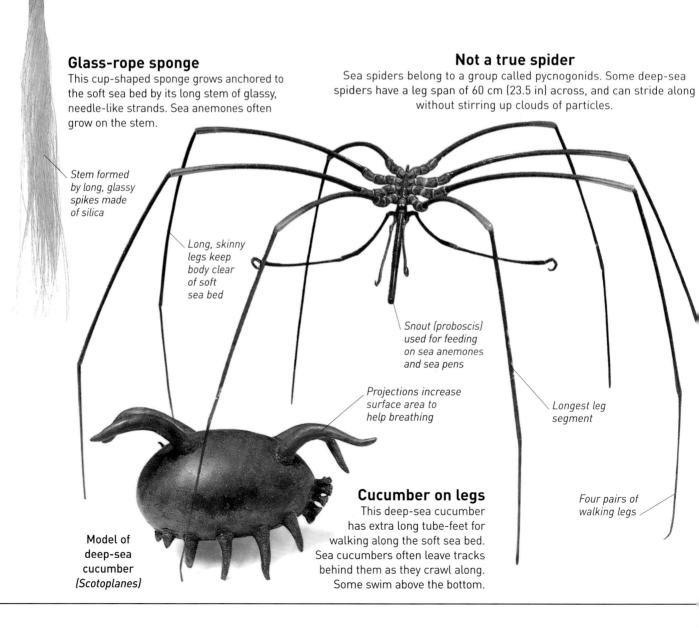

Long, skinny legs keep body clear of soft sea bed

Snout (proboscis) used for feeding on sea anemones and sea pens

Projections increase surface area to help breathing

Longest leg segment

Cucumber on legs
This deep-sea cucumber has extra long tube-feet for walking along the soft sea bed. Sea cucumbers often leave tracks behind them as they crawl along. Some swim above the bottom.

Four pairs of walking legs

Model of deep-sea cucumber (*Scotoplanes*)

Specimens, brought up from the deep, are dried to preserve them

Brittle star's arms wound around sea pen for support

Lily of the deep

Sea lilies use feathery arms to gather food particles from the water. Many live on the deep-sea floor, in trenches that are 100–8,000 m (330–26,000 ft) deep. Some have roots and stems anchored to the sea bed. Those with whorls of spikes (cirri) around their stems can move by using their arms, dragging their stems behind.

Engraving of deep-sea lily

Starting on the bottom

Often called tidal waves, tsunamis are caused by earthquakes or eruptions on the sea bed sending shock waves through the water. The waves race across the open sea. When they near the coast, they bunch up into towering walls of destruction.

Dried deep-sea brittle stars
(Asteronyx loveni)

Long arms can grasp food that drifts by

Stem of sea pen grows up from the sea bed

Flower baskets

The glassy skeletons of Venus flower basket sponges are admired for their beauty, but the living sponge is covered with soft tissues. Most glass sponges live in deep waters, but some live in shallower waters in cold, polar regions.

Opening of sponge covered with sieve plate

Glassy skeleton

All in the arms

These deep-sea brittle stars use long, snake-like arms to cling onto sea pens and to feed on small creatures and other food particles drifting by. Climbing off the sea bed gives them a good chance of collecting food. Brittle stars are common bottom dwellers at any depth, but these deep-sea ones live at 100–1,800 m (330–5,900 ft).

Dried Venus flower basket
(Euplectella aspergillium)

Deep heat

In parts of the ocean floor, very hot, mineral-rich water gushes out. These vents, or hot springs, exist where the gigantic plates that make up Earth's crust are moving apart. Cold seawater sinks deep into cracks where the water is heated. At temperatures of up to 400°C (752°F), hot water spews out, carrying minerals that form chimneys (black smokers). The hot water helps bacteria to grow, which create food from the hydrogen sulphide in the water. These microbes support an extraordinary community of animals.

Crustal plate

Sea floor spreading

Solidified lava makes new crust

Growing ocean

New areas of ocean floor are created at spreading centres between two tectonic plates. When hot, molten rock (lava) emerges from within the crust, the lava cools and hardens, adding material to the edge of both plates. Old areas of ocean floor are destroyed when one plate slides under another.

Black smoker
Animal life abounds in an active vent site, such as this one in the Mid-Atlantic Ridge. If a vent stops producing hot, sulphur-rich water, the community is doomed unless it can find a new site.

Plumes of hot water are rich in sulphides, which are poisonous to most animals

Fish predat nibble tops tube wor

Dense numbers of animals crowd around a vent

Giant clams in the eastern Pacific can grow to 30 cm (12 in) long

Some animals graze on mats of bacteria covering rocks near a vent

Model of hydrothermal vents found in the eastern Pacific

Deep-sea fish photographed from Alvin near a vent on the Mid-Atlantic Ridge

Alvin by the support ship, Atlantis II

Black smoker chimney can reach 10 m (33 ft) high

Chimney made from mineral deposits

Pioneering submersible

The US submersible, *Alvin*, was the first to take scientists down to observe marine life near the Galapagos vents in the east Pacific in the 1970s. Since then, *Alvin* has made many dives to vents around the world to depths of 3,800 m (12,500 ft).

Vent communities

Vent communities vary. This model shows black smokers in the eastern Pacific, where giant clams and tube worms are the most distinctive animals – as are hairy snails in the Mariana Trench and eyeless shrimps along the Mid-Atlantic Ridge.

Tube worm can grow to 3 m (10 ft) long

Giant tube worm has bacteria inside its body, which provide it with food

Diverse divers

People have always wanted to explore the sea, to find wrecks and treasure, study marine life, and (in modern times) drill for oil and gas. The first diving kit was a simple bell containing air. Later, diving suits with hard helmets enabled divers to go deeper and stay longer, with air pumped down a line. In the 1940s, the aqualung or SCUBA (Self-Contained Underwater Breathing Apparatus) enabled divers to carry their air supply in a tank on their back.

Umbilical supplies air and electricity for light

Weight belt

Underwater worker

This diver, wearing a wetsuit for warmth, gets air into the helmet via a line to the surface. A harness around the diver's waist carries tools.

Rope connecting bell to surface

Wooden bell

Weight

Early diving bell

In 1690, Edmund Halley's diving bell allowed divers to be resupplied with barrels of air that were lowered from the surface and linked to the bell and the divers by a tube. The bell, open at the bottom, was used at depths of 18 m (60 ft).

Oxygen flow valve

"Medical lock" for passing liquids and food to diver

Joint pains indicate decompression sickness

Oxygen cylinder

Decompression chamber

Main entrance to decompression chamber

Life saver

The weight of water increases the pressure on the body. If a diver comes up too quickly after a long or deep dive, the sudden drop in pressure can cause the nitrogen in the air supply to form bubbles in the diver's blood and tissues. This painful, sometimes fatal condition is called decompression sickness (the bends). A decompression chamber raises the pressure to move the bubbles out through the lungs, then slowly lowers it to the normal level at the surface.

An early diving suit

classic diving suit

he "Standard" diving suit was
vented by Augustus Siebe in the
330s. Modified versions of this
rd-helmeted suit are still in
se today. The tunic made of
yers of canvas and rubber is
aterproof. The copper and
ass helmet fits onto
heavy breastplate
orselet), which is
lted onto the tunic.
earing heavy boots
d two extra
eights, the diver
ould sink to
epths of about
m (200 ft).

Helmet equipped with two-way communication system so diver can talk to someone on the surface

Weight is about 13 kg (30 lb)

Diver has two weights – one at the front, a second at the back

Helmet made of copper and brass

Face plate

Spanner for tightening bolts on breastplate

Breastplate screwed to tunic using six, eight, or twelve bolts

gjohns made
rom wool for
ater warmth
nd insulation

Complete "Standard" diving suit

Rubber cuff for extra waterproofing

bed cuff
lps trap
arm air

Suit made of a layer of rubber between two layers of canvas

eather boot
h lead base
help weigh
down diver
in water

Each boot weighs 8 kg (18 lb)

Snort mast renews
and expels air with
help of bellows

Augur drills into enemy
ship to attach mine

Delayed
action
mine

Vertical
propeller

Submarines

The first submarines were simple designs
that could travel a short distance under
water and were useful in warfare. Later
versions were powered by diesel or petrol
while on the surface and by batteries
underwater. Since 1955, nuclear power
has allowed submarines to travel great
distances before refuelling. Today, they use
sonar and computer systems to navigate,
track other vessels, and launch missiles.

Side propeller
powered by
foot pedals

"Turtle" hero

A one-man wooden submarine, the *Turtle*, was
used during the American Revolutionary War in
1776 to try to attach a mine to an English ship that
was blockading New York Harbor. The operator
became disorientated by carbon dioxide building
up inside the *Turtle* and jettisoned the bomb.

External
steering bar
operated
by diver

Internal
steering
position

Hand pump for
pressurizing air
reservoir and
emptying
ballast tanks

Underwater adventure

Inspired by the invention of modern
submarines, this 1900 engraving
depicted a scene in the year 2000
with people enjoying a journey in a
submarine liner. Tourists can now
take trips in small submarines to
view marine life in places such as
the Red Sea. However, most people
explore the underwater world by
learning to SCUBA dive or snorkel.

Front wheels
smaller than
back ones for
easier turning

Tower with snort mast, periscope, and radar aerials

Torpedo storage space

Control room

Reactor compartment

Engine room

rpedo tube

Model of HMS *Dreadnought*

Living quarters

Ballast tank takes in water to submerge

Motor generator

Single propeller at tail-end of submarine

Whale-shaped

MS *Dreadnought* had a single propeller at its tail-end. also had a snort mast, while a whale has a blow-hole the top of its head. However, a whale must surface breathe air, whereas HMS *Dreadnought* had an air-onditioning system so its 88-person crew could spend eeks submerged. Operating from 1960 to 1981, it was ritain's first nuclear-powered submarine.

Sperm whale shape on which submarine design is based

Hatch in deck for diver's exit and re-entry

Air reservoir (made from old soda water tank)

ARGONAUT

Inside story
The cramped interior of a submersible has only just enough room for a pilot and perhaps one or two passengers.

Compartment with air lock to maintain enough pressure for diver

Bottom crawler
This model of submersible, called the *Argonaut Junior*, was built in New York in 1894. Powered by a hand-crank, the vehicle was driven over the sea bed at a maximum depth of just 6 m (20 ft). A helmeted diver could leave the craft to pick up oysters, clams, and other objects. A metal tank contained the diver's air supply, and a garden hose linked the tank to the helmet.

Model of American submersible from the late 1800s, the *Argonaut Junior*

Ocean explorers

Microscope used by a marine biologist in Scotland during the late 1800s

Image from 1900 of a submarine bus in 200[...]

The ocean has always been a place of mystery, with little to see on the surface. The first depth soundings were made by dropping a lead weight on a line until the operator felt it hit the bottom. Echo sounders, invented during World War I, bounced pulses of sound off the sea bed. This led to sonar systems that could map the ocean floor. For centuries, the only clues to deep-sea life were creatures brought up in fishermen's nets or washed ashore. In the 1870s, HMS *Challenger*'s trawls showed that the deep ocean did contain life. Today, manned and unmanned submersibles reach otherwise inaccessible waters. Even so, much of the ocean is yet to be explored.

Gloria at work

To survey the sea bed, GLORIA was towed behind its mother ship at a speed of 10 knots. Sound pulses from GLORIA would span across the sea bed for up to 30 km (18 miles) on each side. GLORIA picked up echoes bouncing back from features on the sea bed. These were processed by on-board computers to produce maps of the sea floor.

Glorious GLORIA

GLORIA, for Geological Long Range Inclined Asdic (sonar), was used to survey the ocean floor. Covering 20,000 sq km (7,700 sq miles) in a day, GLORIA scanned more than five per cent of the world's oceans in 20 years.

Cradle's hydraulic system tipped GLORIA into the water

Inside GLORIA are two rows of transducers, which emit sounds (sonar pulses)

Rope guide, used during recovery of GLORIA

Cable drum

GLORIA was towed by the nose

Torpedo-shaped body (towfish) is 8 m (26 ft) long and weighs about 2 tonnes (2.2 US tons)

Launching cradle weighs about 13 tonne[...] (14.3 US tons)

Cable, 400 m (1,300 ft) long, contains electrical wiring for signalling

Snorkelling

A simple way to observe life underwater is to snorkel just below the surface. The swimmer breathes through a snorkel that sticks out above water.

Air expelled through end of snorkel

Fins propel swimmer along, but arms should be kept near the body for streamlining

Scuba diver looking at grouper fish in the Red Sea

Face mask traps air to let swimmer view life in the water

Swimmer breathes in air and expels it through mouthpiece

SCUBA diving

SCUBA equipment has proved invaluable in the study of marine life in shallow waters. Instead of bringing animals into an aquarium, marine biologists can observe them in the wild.

Snorkel tube

Deep stars

Many submersibles have been used for underwater exploration. The deepest dive ever was to 10,912 m (35,800 ft) in the Mariana Trench in 1960.

Deep Star can reach depths of 1,200 m (4,000 ft)

Fins used in snorkelling and SCUBA diving

Autosub

This Autonomous Underwater Vehicle (AUV) can explore remote parts of the ocean. AUVs are unmanned and operate without being tethered to a ship or submersible.

Autosub uses a suite of sensors to collect data

Mechanical arm used to lower Autosub into the water

Wrecks on the sea bed

Ever since people took to the sea in boats, there have been wrecks on the sea bed. Mud and sand cover wooden hulls, protecting the timbers by keeping out the oxygen which speeds up decay. Metal-hulled ships are badly corroded by seawater; the *Titanic*'s steel hull could disintegrate within a hundred years. Wrecks in shallow water get covered by plant and animal life, turning them into living reefs. Uncovering wrecks and their objects can tell us much about life in the past.

Less valuable silver coin

Glittering gold
Spanish coins, much in demand by pirates, sometimes ended up on the sea bed when a ship sank.

Sonar equipment

Titanium sphere

IFR
DCN

Super sub
The French submersible, *Nautile*, recovered objects from the sea bed surrounding the wreck of the *Titanic*. Only a submersible could dive deep enough to reach the wreck, 3,780 m (2.5 miles) down. The *Nautile* takes about 90 minutes to reach the site, and can stay down for eight hours. The pilot, co-pilot, and observer sit in a small sphere made of titanium metal, which protects them from the huge pressure at these depths.

Valuable property
In 1892, divers worked on the wreck of the tug *L'Abeille*, off Le Havre, France, to bring up (salvage) items of value.

Lights for video camera

Manipulator arm for picking objects off sea bed

Sad reminders
Many items recovered from the *Titanic* wreck were not valuable, but everyday items such as this cutlery remind us of those who used them before they died.

The unsinkable ship
In 1912, the *Titanic* sailed from England to New York on her maiden voyage. When she hit an iceberg, she took 2 hours and 40 minutes to sink, with only 705 people saved out of 2,228. The wreck was found in 1985 by a French-US team, using remote-controlled video equipment on an unmanned probe.

Plane wreck

This Japanese biplane crashed into the sea off Papua New Guinea in the Pacific. The Bermuda Triangle in the Atlantic is famous for the many planes that mysteriously vanished there.

Sunken treasure

These precious jewels are among many valuable items salvaged from the wreck of the Spanish galleon, the *Tolossa*, in the 1970s. Bound for Mexico in 1724, she foundered on a massive coral reef during a hurricane. Such treasure shows that the Spanish exported luxury goods to their New World colonies.

Gold, diamonds, and pearls from the wreck of the Tolossa off Hispaniola

Nautile measures 8 m (26 ft) in length

Thruster propels Nautile forwards

Encrusted Roman jar

Barnacle

Mollusc shell

Lost continent

This film poster shows the mythical land of Atlantis sinking beneath the sea. In fact a Greek island did sink beneath the waves after an earthquake in c. 1600 BCE.

Sea bed home

Barnacle shells and worm tubes grew on this Roman jar while it rested for hundreds of years on the sea bed. Archaeologists try to survey, raise, and clean such objects without damaging them.

Worm tube

Harvesting fish

More than 90 million tonnes of fish are caught around the world each year. Some fish are caught by hand-thrown nets and traps in local waters, but far more are caught at sea by fishing vessels using the latest technology. Some fish are caught on long lines with many hooks, or ensnared when they swim into long walls of drift nets. Using sonar to detect shoals means there are few places where fish can escape notice, even at 1,000 m (3,300 ft). If too many fish are caught, however, stocks take a long time to recover.

1 Hatching out
Salmon begin life in rivers and streams. The fry (alevins) hatch from eggs laid in a shallow hollow among gravel and feed on the egg sac.

2 Young salmon
At a few weeks old, the egg sac disappears, so young salmon must feed on tiny insects in the river. The young salmon (called parr) stay in the river for a year or more, before turning into silvery smolt, which head for the sea.

3 At sea
Atlantic salmon spend up to four years at sea, feeding on other fishes and putting on several kilos annually. Then the mature salmon return to the home rivers and streams where they hatched. They recognize their home stream by a number of clues, including the water's "smell".

Fin rays are well-developed

Large, first dorsal fin

Pelvic fin

Pectoral fin

Operculum (flap covering gills)

Teeth for gripping slippery prey

Fish farming
To meet the demand for fish, young salmon are reared in fresh water and then released into pens in calm sea waters, such as sea lochs. To help them grow quickly, they are fed with dried fish pellets. However, parasites called sea lice, common among farmed salmon, are infecting and killing wild salmon.

Sockeye salmon from the Pacific

Symmetrical caudal (tail) fin

Body inflates, making it hard for a predator to grab it

⌐reeding colours
⌐s adult salmon swim upriver to spawn, they change ⌐olour and the females become swollen with eggs.

Small, second dorsal fin

Deadly meal
Puffer fish, sometimes known as blowfish, are a delicacy in Japan, but the flesh must be prepared carefully because certain parts of the body contain a deadly poison.

Anal fin

Engraving of an Atlantic cod

In peril
Atlantic cod are a favourite in the British dish of fish and chips, but many stocks are overfished and severely depleted.

Purse seine nets let out in mid-water around a shoal of fish

When shoal surrounded, the bottom of the net is closed and it is dragged onto boat

Heavy boards on each side keep net open

⌐Weights at ⌐ottom and floats at top of net help keep it straight

Trawl net

Fish are caught in end of net

Purse seine nets

Bottom trawls sweep along sea bed

⌐ the net
⌐his old-style steam-engine trawler ⌐shed in the northern Atlantic in ⌐e 1940s and 1950s, pitching ⌐ts over the side. Modern, ⌐ore efficient trawlers ⌐wer bigger nets ⌐om the back of ⌐e boat.

Mizzen light

Hanging blocks for trawl net ropes

John Henry, a side trawler from Grimsby, England

Deck lights for night fishing

Funnel

Lifeboat

Trawl winch

JOHN HENRY GY.000

GY.000

Ocean products

People have always harvested plants and animals from the ocean, from fish, crustaceans (shrimps, lobsters), and molluscs (clams, squid) to sea cucumbers and seaweeds. Most are collected for food, although some sea animals and seaweeds are now cultivated to meet demand for products and to avoid over-collecting the ocean's wildlife. Some sea creatures are made into amazing products, however many (such as mother-of-pearl buttons) are now replaced by synthetic materials.

Yarn dyed purple from pigment of sea snails

Royal purple
Sea snails were used to make a purple dye for clothes worn by kings in ancient times. The liquid was extracted from huge quantities of salted snails left in vats gouged out of rocks, then heated to concentrate the dye.

Slate-pencil sea urchin from tropical coral reefs in the Indo-Pacific

Short, blunt spines surround mouth

Useful spines
The spines of this sea urchin were once used as pencils to write on slate boards. Slate-pencil urchins are still collected, their spines used for wind chimes. Urchins use their big spines to help them walk across the sea bed when they leave their crevices to feed at night

Long, very strong spines help protect urchin from predators

Spines help urchin move and to hold it in place

Five, strong white teeth protrude from urchin's mouth (viewed from underneath)

Soft skeleton left after processing living sponge

Soft skeleton
Bath sponges grow among sea grasses in reef lagoons. When brought up from the sandy sea bed, the sponges are covered with slimy, living tissues. Natural sponges are prone to diseases and over-collecting.

Seaweed farm
In Japan, seaweeds are used in crackers and to wrap raw fish parcels. Red seaweed is grown on bamboo poles, collected, and dried. The seaweed's jelly-like agar is used in foods and medical research. Seaweeds are also used as fertilizers.

Shiny pearls

Pearls are produced by mussels and oysters in response to irritation. Natural pearls form around a piece of grit that gets between the oyster's shell and its skin (mantle). Tissues from the mantle surround the grit and produce mother-of-pearl layers. Pearls are cultivated by inserting particles into a clam.

Double strand of blue pearls

Gloves can be made from byssus threads of noble pen shell

Shell can close to protect itself from predators

Salt pans

When seawater evaporates, a salt-crystal crust is left behind. Large quantities of sea salt are produced by flooding shallow ponds (pans) with seawater and letting the water evaporate in the hot Sun. Sea salt is produced in places with warm weather and little rain.

Noble pen shell grows to 60 cm (24 in) in length

Silver cross inlaid with abalone shell

Tapered shell is brittle

Hole to expel water and waste

Byssus threads made by shell to anchor it to sea bed

Golden threads

In the Mediterranean, the pen shell produces a thick mat of byssus threads. These threads were once collected, spun into fine, golden thread, and then woven into cloth. Perhaps this cloth started the Ancient Greek legend of the golden fleece.

Rainbow hues

Inside an abalone shell are all the colours of the rainbow. The heavy shell's mother-of-pearl is used to make jewellery and buttons. These shells are popular with New Zealand's Maoris. Abalones are also eaten.

Oil and gas

Valuable reservoirs of oil and gas lie hidden beneath the sea bed. Only certain kinds of rocks hold oil and gas, but must be in shallow enough water to be reached by drilling. Geologists find the reservoirs by sending shock waves through the sea bed and using the returning signals to distinguish between the rock layers. Temporary rigs are set up to see if the oil is of the right quality and quantity. To extract oil or gas, the rig is replaced by a more permanent oil platform, which is firmly anchored to the sea bed. Oil can be piped ashore or stored on floating vessels (FPSOs) until it is loaded onto tankers.

Impermeable rock stops oil moving up

Oil is trapped in porous, reservoir rock

Porous rock lets oil pass through

Death and decay
Plant and bacteria remains fell to the ancient sea bed and were covered by layers of mud. Heat and pressure turned them into oil, then gas, which rises.

Wind turbines
Oil reservoirs run dry, but wind turbines are a source of renewable energy. This wind farm operates off North Wales, UK.

Tallest structure on this platform is flare stack for safety reasons

At work
Platform workers check the drill bit that is used to cut through the rock. Special mud is sent down pipes to cool the bit, wash out the ground up rock, and prevent the oil from gushing out.

On fire
Oil and gas are highly flammable. Accidents such as the North Sea's *Piper Alpha* disaster in 1988, when 167 people died, have led to improved safety measures.

Floating production
Floating vessels called FPSOs (Floating Production, Storage, Offloading) store the oil and gas produced from nearby drilling platforms and undersea wells until it is taken away by tankers. FPSOs work well in deepwater locations that are too far to connect to the shore by sea-bed pipelines. They can also move out of the way of hurricanes or drifting icebergs.

FPSO GIRASSOL

Newt suit

A thick-walled suit resists pressure. When underwater, the diver breathes air at normal pressure as if inside a submersible. This allows a diver to go deeper without having to undergo decompression (p. 48). Newt suits (left) are used in oil exploration to depths of 365 m (1,200 ft).

Milk round

Helicopters deliver crew and supplies to oil platforms far out at sea. Up to 400 people can live and work on an oil platform, including geologists, cooks, and the mechanics who look after the machinery.

On the bottom

Divers (minus Newt suits), doing repairs underwater, work longer if they return to a pressurized chamber, then back into the sea, without having to decompress after each dive.

Helicopter pad – fresh food and milk are flown in

Living quarters

Fireproof lifeboat gives better chance of survival

Strong structure to withstand buffeting by wind and waves

ER UNDERWATER HAZARD

Jewellery made of teeth of great white shark, now vulnerable

Oceans in peril

Oceans and ocean life are under threat. Overharvesting has depleted many ocean animals, from whales to fishes, while sewage and industrial waste are dumped into the sea, carrying chemicals that disrupt the food chain. Oil spills smother and poison marine life. Nets and rubbish dumped at sea can choke turtles or trap birds. Today, laws help to stop ocean pollution and protect marine life.

Cut to show mother-of-pearl

Have a heart
Prized for their beauty, most shells sold in shops have been taken as living animals. But if too many creatures are taken from one place, such as a coral reef, the pattern of life can be disrupted. Instead of buying shells, it is better to go beachcombing and collect the empty shells of already dead creatures. Always check first, as some nature reserves do not permit this.

Heart cockle shells

Oil spill
Oil is needed for industry and motor vehicles. Huge quantities are brought up from the sea bed, transported in tankers, and sent along pipelines. Accidents happen where massive amounts of oil are spilled. Oil-soaked seabirds and sea mammals die of cold, because their feathers or fur no longer contain pockets of air to keep them warm.

Saving beauty
This chambered nautilus shell was carved in the 17th century. The six kinds of nautilus in the Pacific and Indian oceans are at risk from over-collecting. They are hunted at night when they rise to the surface. Chambered nautili grow quite slowly, reaching maturity in six or more years, so populations can take a long time to recover.

Worse for whales

For centuries, whales have been hunted for their meat, oil, and bones. Whale oil was used in foods, as lubricants, and in soap and candles, and the broad baleen plates were made into household items such as brushes. Commercial whaling drastically reduced whale numbers. Most kinds of whales are now protected, but some are still caught for food.

Oily whale meat extract, for margarine

Ground whale meal, for animal feed

Whale liver oil, a source of vitamin A

Sperm oil, a lubricant for motor cars

Japanese painting showing early whalers in small boats risking their lives in pursuit of whales

Engraved nautilus shell

Intricate floral pattern cut into shell

Sponges settled on scrap iron in Red Sea harbour

Take care

Sea life is fragile. A basket sponge this size may be 100 years old, but could be damaged by a diver's kick. All kinds of junk on the sea bed (centre, right) is smothering marine life. In the 1997–98 El Niño, sea temperatures rose by 1–2°C (2–4°F) in parts of the Indian Ocean, causing some corals to eject their algae partners and die. Many scientists think global warming may have contributed to the unusual temperature rise.

Did you know?

FASCINATING FACTS

★ The world's oceans contain 97% of Earth's water. Of the remaning 3%, just over 2% is locked in ice, and just under 1% is freshwater.

Tiny cleaner wrasse at work inside the mouth of a grouper fish

★ The coldest sea surface is in the White Sea, in the Arctic, at –2°C (28.4°F). The warmest is in summer in shallow parts of the Indian Ocean's Persian Gulf, at 35.6°C (96.1°F).

★ The temperature of the oceans' deepest water is between 2 and 4°C (34–39°F).

★ The highest mountain underwater is in the Pacific Ocean, near New Zealand. At 8.7 km (5.4 miles) tall, it is nearly as high as Mount Everest, Earth's highest mountain.

★ The greatest tidal range and the highest tides in the world occur in Canada's Bay of Fundy, in the Atlantic, where the difference between low and high tides can be up to 16 m (52 ft).

Pacific Ocean as seen from space

★ The Pacific Ocean, at 153 million sq km (59 million sq miles) covers about one-third of Earth's surface.

★ Ninety per cent of all marine life occurs in the sunlit, or euphotic, zone – the surface layer of the ocean where there is enough light to support photosynthesis. Here, plankton provide the basis of the ocean's food chain.

★ A bucket of seawater can contain up to 10 million phytoplankton and zooplankton. Most phytoplankton are less than 0.01 mm (0.0003 in) wide.

★ The largest meat-eating fish is the great white shark. Some grow up to 6 m (20 ft) long and weigh around 1.5 tonnes (1.65 US tons).

★ A great white shark can detect one part of blood from a wounded animal in 100 million parts of water.

★ To flee predators, flying fish can leap 2 m (6 ft) out of the water and "fly" 100 m (325 ft) on outspread fins.

★ At birth, a blue whale can weigh about 3 tonnes (3.3 US tons). The babies guzzle 100 litres (180 pints) of their mother's milk a day and grow at almost 5 kg (11 lb) an hour.

★ Small fish called cleaner wrasse feed on parasites that infest much larger fish, such as a grouper, even swimming right inside the larger fish's mouth to feed.

Spines flattened against body

Porcupine fish at its normal size...

Body spines stick out

... and when inflated

★ If threatened, a porcupine fish takes in water to swell its body to twice its normal size, making it too large and uncomfortable to swallow.

Plankton magnified several hundred times

QUESTIONS AND ANSWERS

Q Why is the sea salty?

A Salt is washed out of Earth's rock, sand, and soils by rainwater, then carried in streams and rivers to the sea. Over millions of years, this has built up the sea's concentration of salt.

Waves forming out at sea

Q What causes waves?

A Most waves are created by the wind blowing across the ocean. Their height depends on the strength and duration of the wind.

Q Why is the sea blue?

A Blue light from sunlight is the least absorbed by clear seawater. When sunlight enters the water, the blue light is scattered and some is reflected back to the surface.

Q How many types of fish are there?

A There are around 25,000 species of marine and freshwater fish. Around 24,000 are bony fishes, 1,100 are cartilaginous or gristly fishes and about 100 are jawless fishes.

Larger upper tail vane

Tail vanes equal in size

Cartilaginous fish – blacktip reef shark (top) and bony fish – mackerel (above)

Q How do cartilaginous and bony fish differ?

A Bony fish have bony skeletons, while sharks and rays have skeletons made of cartilage (gristle). Bony fish also have a gas-filled swim bladder to control buoyancy, so they remain still. Gristly fish will start to sink if they don't keep moving. Bony fish have tail vanes of equal size and protective gill flaps, whereas most sharks have larger upper tail vanes than lower ones, and gill slits without flaps.

Stargazer hiding in gravel on the sea bed

Q How do fish hide from predators in the open sea?

A Fish that live near the surface have dark backs and paler bellies that help to camouflage them from above and below. Fish on the sea bed can blend in with their surroundings.

Record Breakers

★ **LARGEST SEA CREATURE**
The blue whale is the world's largest animal, at up to 30 m (98 ft) long and as much as 150 tonnes (165 US tons) in weight.

★ **BIGGEST FISH**
The whale shark can grow up to 12.65 m (41.5 ft) and weigh 20 tonnes (22 US tons).

★ **SMALLEST FISH**
The adult Marshall Islands dwarf goby is just 6 mm (0.3 in) from nose to tail.

★ **HEAVIEST BONY FISH**
The ocean sunfish, or *Mola mola*, can weigh up to 2 tonnes (2.2 US tons).

★ **FASTEST FISH**
The sailfish can reach speeds of up to 109 kph (68 mph) – faster than a cheetah can run.

Whale shark

The world's oceans

There are five oceans. The Pacific, Atlantic, Indian, and Arctic oceans fill natural basins in Earth's crust. The Southern Ocean is technically part of the southern Pacific, Atlantic, and Indian oceans but is officially delimited from them south of 60 degrees latitude.

PACIFIC OCEAN

The Pacific Ocean is the world's largest ocean, covering 28% of Earth's surface. It has 20,000–30,000 islands, and is surrounded by a "Ring of Fire", where tectonic activity causes frequent eruptions and quakes.

AREA: 152,617,160 sq km (58,957,258 sq miles)

Includes: Bali Sea, Bering Sea, Bering Strait, Coral Sea, East China Sea, Florest Sea, Gulf of Alaska, Gulf of Tonkin, Java Sea, Philippine Sea, Savu Sea, Sea of Japan, Sea of Okhotsk, South China Sea, Tasman Sea, Timor Sea

AVERAGE DEPTH: 4,229 m (13,874 ft)

DEEPEST POINT: 11,034 m (36,201 ft) Challenger Deep in the Mariana Trench

COASTLINE: 135,663 km (84,299 miles)

Unmanned sub reached bottom of the Mariana Trench in 1995

Kaiko submersible

CLIMATE: Strong currents and trade winds constantly blow across the Pacific's waters, often causing violent tropical storms.

NATURAL RESOURCES: Fish stocks, oil and gas fields, sand and gravel aggregates.

Coral atoll reef in the southwest Pacific

ENVIRONMENTAL ISSUES: Nearly half of the world's shipping routes cross the Pacific, including huge supertankers, bulk carriers, and container ships. As a result, the ocean suffers from oil pollution, which threatens marine life and seabirds. Some of the Pacific's endangered marine creatures include dugongs, sea otters, sea lions, seals, turtles, and whales.

ATLANTIC OCEAN

The Atlantic is the world's second-largest ocean, covering about one-fifth of Earth's surface. An underwater mountain chain called the Mid-Atlantic Ridge runs down its centre.

Panama Canal links Atlantic and Pacific

AREA: 81,527,400 sq km (31,477,905 sq miles)

Includes: Baltic Sea, Black Sea, Caribbean Sea, Davis Strait, Denmark Strait, Gulf of Guinea, Gulf of Mexico, Labrador Sea, Mediterranean Sea, North Sea, Norwegian Sea, Sargasso Sea, Scotia Sea

AVERAGE DEPTH: 3,777 m (12,391 ft)

DEEPEST POINT: 8,605 m (28,232 ft) Milwaukee Deep in the Puerto Rico Trench

COASTLINES: 111,866 km (69,512 miles)

CLIMATE: Northerly waters are usually covered with sea ice in winter. The Gulf Stream, a warm water current, flows from the Gulf of Mexico, north and then east, which raises the temperatures of northern Europe and keeps many northern ports ice-free during the winter.

NATURAL RESOURCES: Fish, oil, gas, sand, gravel.

ENVIRONMENTAL ISSUES: Some Atlantic waters are polluted by industrial waste, sewage, and oil. Fish stocks have run low because of overfishing, especially with trawling for bottom-living fish, such as cod.

Atlantic trawler

INDIAN OCEAN

The Indian Ocean is the world's third-largest ocean. Its northern currents flow southwest along the coast of Somalia in winter and in the opposite direction in summer.

Endangered green turtle

AREA: 67,469,536 sq km (26,050,133 sq miles)

Includes: Andaman Sea, Arabian Sea, Bay of Bengal, Great Australian Bight, Gulf of Aden, Gulf of Oman, Java Sea, Mozambique Channel, Persian Gulf, Red Sea, Strait of Malacca, Timor Sea

AVERAGE DEPTH: 3,877 m (12,720 ft)

DEEPEST POINT: 7,125 m (23,376 ft) Java Trench, also called Sunda Trench

COASTLINE: 66,526 km (41,338 miles)

CLIMATE: Cool dry winds blow from the northeast in February and March. In August and September, southwesterly winds bring monsoon rain and flooding.

NATURAL RESOURCES: Oil and gas fields, sand and gravel, fish.

ENVIRONMENTAL ISSUES: Oil pollution; endangered sea life includes the dugong, turtles, and whales.

Oil production in the Arabian Sea

ARCTIC OCEAN

The Arctic Ocean is the world's smallest ocean. Between December and May, most of the ocean is covered by polar ice.

AREA: 8,676,520 sq km (3,350,023 sq miles)

Includes: Baffin Bay, Barents Sea, Beaufort Sea, Chukchi Sea, East Siberian Sea, Greenland Sea, Hudson Bay, Kara Sea, Laptev Sea, Northwest Passage

AVERAGE DEPTH: 1,935 m (6,349 ft)

DEEPEST POINT: 5,680 m (18,635 ft) Fram Basin

COASTLINE: 45,389 km (28,203 miles)

Steel-hulled ice breakers crush ice and open up a lane for other ships

CLIMATE: Polar, with continuous cold and narrow annual temperature ranges.

NATURAL RESOURCES: Oil and gas, sand and gravel, fish, marine mammals.

ENVIRONMENTAL ISSUES: Loss of sea ice due to climate change.

Polar bear

Partly webbed front paws for swimming

SOUTHERN OCEAN

The Southern Ocean is the world's fourth-largest ocean. Parts of the ocean freeze in winter, forming the vast Ronne and Ross ice shelves.

AREA: 20,973,318 sq km (8,097,843 sq miles)

Includes: Amundsen, Bellingshausen, Ross, and Weddell seas

AVERAGE DEPTH: 4,500 m (14,760 ft)

DEEPEST POINT: 7,235 m (23,737 ft) South Sandwich Trench

COASTLINE: 17,968 km (11,165 miles)

CLIMATE: Polar, with continuous cold and narrow annual temperature ranges.

NATURAL RESOURCES: Probable large oil and gas fields, sand, gravel, fish, krill.

ENVIRONMENTAL ISSUES: Ultraviolet radiation penetrating through the ozone hole above the Antarctic is damaging phytoplankton. Despite treaties, illegal and unregulated fishing still occurs, but protected whale and fur seal populations are making a comeback after over-hunting in the 18th and 19th centuries.

Characteristic flat-topped Antarctic iceberg

Statistics compiled from data from the Naval Oceanographic Office, Stennis Space Centre, Mississippi (2001)

Find out more

There is a wealth of information available about the oceans and marine life. If you do not live (or go on holiday) near the sea, your first stop should be an aquarium. Look out, also, for excellent wildlife programmes on television, or search the Internet using the websites listed below as a starting point.

Razor shell encrusted with barnacles, oyster (behind), and slipper limpet

Sea shells

If you visit the beach, look out for sea shells washed up on the shore. Bring a guidebook to help you identify them. Always put inhabited shells back where you find them, and never collect shells from a protected site. Removing shells can damage the ecosystem.

Visit an aquarium

Plan a visit to an aquarium to observe a huge range of marine life from all over the world. Many aquariums have impressive viewing tanks containing hundreds of species, from jellyfish and octopuses to sharks and starfish. Look out for special events where you can get up close to sharks, rays, and other marine creatures.

USEFUL WEBSITES

- Marine Life Information Network:
  www.marlin.ac.uk
- News and interactive information on the oceans:
  www.oceanlink.info
- Find out what you can do to help the ocean:
  www.mcsuk.org
- Homepage of the Monterey Bay Aquarium, with live web cams:
  www.montereybayaquarium.org

Study a rock pool

Rock pools are fascinating microhabitats, filled with a wide variety of plants and animals. Even if you visit the same rock pool several times, it is unlikely you will find the same creatures. Look out for starfish, anemones, mussels, and seaweed, such as sea lettuce and kelp. If you keep fairly still, you may also spot crabs hiding in crevices between rocks, or a tiny fish.

Face to face

You can see marine life close up if you take a trip in a glass-bottomed boat or a tourist submarine. Or try snorkelling – it's amazing what you can see once you're below the ocean's surface, especially if you snorkel over a coral reef.

Flukes (tail parts) of a humpback whale

Whale watching

Various companies organize whale-watching tours, giving you the chance of seeing whales in their natural environment. The tourists pictured left are observing humpback whales off the coast of Alaska.

Marine sanctuaries

Marine sanctuaries are established to protect local wildlife and educate the public about the marine environment. Why not plan a trip to a sanctuary or find out more about them through the Internet. You can also join organizations working to protect and conserve the world's oceans.

Otter in the Monterey Bay National Marine Sanctuary, off the coast of California, USA

PLACES TO VISIT

LONDON AQUARIUM, LONDON, UK

Has over 65 displays and 500 species, and includes:
• vast glass tanks, each descending over three floors, displaying marine life in the Pacific and Atlantic oceans
• Gentoo penguins, snorkelling with sharks, turtle feeding

THE DEEP, HULL, UK

Includes over 100 species of marine fish and features:
• one of the deepest display tanks in Europe, descending 10 m (33 ft) and including several species of shark
• displays of marine life in different environments, from coral lagoons to the twilight zones and the polar oceans

DEEP SEA WORLD, NORTH QUEENSFERRY, FIFE, UK

Scotland's national aquarium, featuring:
• the world's longest underwater safari tunnel
• dives with sharks

MARY ROSE MARITIME MUSEUM, PORTSMOUTH, UK

The Tudor flagship's museum, with:
• exhibits on the ship's salvage and restoration
• displays of artefacts and crew's personal possessions

Pewter jug from the Mary Rose

Glossary

Bioluminescence

ABYSSAL PLAIN The flat floor of an ocean basin covered in a layer of sediment. (*see also* BASIN, SEDIMENT)

ANTARCTIC Region at the South Pole, south of the Antarctic Circle.

ARCTIC Region at the North Pole, north of the Arctic Circle.

ATOLL Coral reef surrounding a lagoon, growing on the rim of a volcanic island that has sunk.

BASIN Large, natural bowl-shaped indentation in Earth's crust. Four of the world's oceans lie in such basins.

BIOLUMINESCENCE Meaning living (bio) light (luminescence) – the production of light by a living organism. Some deep-sea creatures produce their own light. In others, it is produced by bacteria living in them.

BIVALVE Soft-bodied animal living in a hinged shell, such as a clam or oyster.

BLACK SMOKER Tall, chimney-like vent on the ocean floor that belches out super-hot water containing chemicals used by some deep-sea creatures to make food. Black smokers occur at volcanically active spots on mid-ocean ridges. (*see also* MID-OCEAN RIDGE)

BONY FISH Fish such as mackerel or cod with a bony skeleton and a swim bladder to control buoyancy.

CARTILAGINOUS FISH Fish such as a shark or ray, with a gristly or cartilaginous skeleton and no swim bladder, meaning it will sink if it doesn't keep moving.

CEPHALOPOD Type of mollusc with a soft body and suckered tentacles, such as a squid or octopus.

CONTINENTAL CRUST The parts of Earth's crust that form the continents.

CONTINENTAL DRIFT Theory that Earth's continents were once a single mass of land that slowly drifted apart over millions of years, and are still moving today.

CONTINENTAL SHELF Sloping submerged land at a continent's edge.

CONTINENTAL SLOPE Sloping submerged land that descends from the continental shelf to the abyssal plain, forming the side of an ocean basin. (*see also* ABYSSAL PLAIN, BASIN)

COPEPOD Tiny, shrimp-like creature, forming part of the ocean's zooplankton. (*see also* ZOOPLANKTON)

CRUSTACEAN Animal, such as a crab or krill, with jointed legs and a tough, jointed outer skeleton over its body.

Krill

CURRENT Body of water that flows through the sea; there are both surface and deep water currents.

DARK ZONE Area of the ocean bordered by the twilight zone above and the abyss below, from around 1,000–4,000 m (3,300–13,200 ft) deep. Also called the bathypelagic zone.

DIATOM Single-celled alga and type of phytoplankton that floats near the ocean's surface, forming the basis of an ocean food chain or food web; common in cool waters.

DORSAL FIN Fin on the back of a fish that helps it keep its balance as it swims.

ECHINODERM Marine invertebrate with spines in the skin, such as a starfish.

EL NIÑO Warm water current that flows east towards the western coast of South America every few years, causing worldwide weather changes.

FOOD CHAIN Series or group of plants and animals linked by their feeding relationships. A food chain usually includes algae, or plants, plant-eating animals, and meat-eating animals.

FOOD WEB A series of several interlinked food chains.

HURRICANE Tropical storm with winds of more than 119 kph (74 mph), forming over the Atlantic Ocean. Tropical storms are usually called typhoons in the Pacific Ocean and cyclones in the Indian Ocean.

ICEBERG Floating mass of ice broken off an ice-sheet or glacier, carried along by ocean currents.

INVERTEBRATE Animal without a backbone.

Swirling winds of a hurricane forming over the Atlantic

Starfish (an echinoderm)

KRILL Shrimp-like crustacean that lives in Arctic and Antarctic waters in great numbers, forming much of the food supply of baleen whales.

MAGMA Molten rock that lies beneath the Earth's crust.

MARINE BIOLOGY The study of ocean life.

MID-OCEAN RIDGE Long, undersea mountain range forming where two tectonic plates are pulling apart, with magma rising from beneath Earth's surface and hardening into rock.

MOLLUSC An invertebrate with a soft body usually enclosed by a shell. Includes bivalves (such as clams), gastropods (such as sea slugs), and cephalopods (such as squid and octopuses). (*see also* BIVALVE, CEPHALOPOD)

OCEANOGRAPHY The scientific study of the oceans.

PHYTOPLANKTON Microscopic single-celled algae that drift in the ocean's sunlit zone. (*see also* SUNLIT ZONE)

PLANKTON Tiny plant and animal organisms that drift in surface waters and are the basis of most marine food chains. (*see also* FOOD CHAIN, ZOOPLANKTON)

PLATE TECTONICS The study of the movement of the lithospheric plates that carry the oceanic and continental crust.

POLYP A sea anemone or coral with a mouth surrounded by tentacles. A hard coral polyp makes a limestone cup, or skeleton, to protect its body. Thousands of polyps live together in colonies, forming a coral reef.

ROV Short for Remotely Operated Vehicle – a small vessel operated from (and tethered to) a submersible or ship.

SALINITY The amount of dissolved salt in seawater. Salinity is measured as parts of salt per 1,000 parts of seawater; the average salinity of the oceans is 35 parts of salt per 1,000 parts of seawater.

SCUBA Stands for Self-Contained Underwater Breathing Apparatus – SCUBA divers carry their own air supply in tanks on their backs.

SEA Another word for ocean, or a particular part of an ocean – for example, the Black Sea and the Mediterranean Sea are connected to the Atlantic Ocean.

SEAMOUNT Underwater volcano that rises 1,000 m (3,280 ft) or more above the surrounding plain.

SEDIMENT Mud, sand, and silt, containing millions of tiny plants and animals, washed off the land by rivers. Sediment settles on the ocean floor.

SONAR Short for Sound Navigation And Ranging – a system that can locate the position of an object by emitting sounds then timing the echoes that bounce back.

SUBMERSIBLE Manned or remotely operated underwater research submarine designed to withstand water pressure in deep water. (*see also* WATER PRESSURE)

SUNLIT ZONE Surface layer of the ocean penetrated by sunlight, to around 200 m (660 ft) deep. Most marine life lives here. Also called the epipelagic zone.

SYMBIOSIS Close interaction between two different species where either, both, or neither benefit from the relationship.

Black smoker

TIDE The regular rise and fall of the sea caused by the gravitational pull of the Sun and the Moon on our planet.

TRENCH A steep-sided trough or valley in the ocean floor.

TSUNAMI Sea wave usually caused by an underwater volcanic eruption or earthquake. It can cause great damage if it reaches the coast as it may gain considerable height in shallow water. Sometimes wrongly called a tidal wave, a tsunami has no connection to the tide.

TWILIGHT ZONE Area of the ocean from around 200 –1,000 m (660–3,300 ft) deep, bordered by the sunlit zone above and darkness below. Also called the mesopelagic zone.

Submersible

TYPHOON Name given to a tropical storm in the western Pacific Ocean. (*see also* HURRICANE)

UPWELLING Rising of cool, nutrient-rich water from deeper parts of the ocean to the surface, where phytoplankton and other marine life gather to feed. (*see also* PHYTOPLANKTON)

WATER PRESSURE Force exerted by water because of its weight and density; water pressure increases by one atmosphere for each 10 m (33 ft) depth.

WAVE HEIGHT The distance between the crest (top of a wave) and its trough (lowest part of a wave).

WAVELENGTH The vertical distance between two successive wave crests (the tops of the waves).

ZOOPLANKTON Tiny animals that float in the water, such as copepods and tiny crustaceans, forming part of plankton. (*see also* PHYTOPLANKTON, PLANKTON)

Index

A

abalone 59
abyssal plain 9, 10, 70;
 Demerara 9;Hatteras 9;
 Nares 9
algae 20, 22, 24, 25, 63, 70
Alvin 47
anemone, cloak 31;
 Dahlia 29; sea 10, 24,
 29, 30, 31, 44
archaeology, underwater,
 54–55
Argonaut Junior 51
Asteronyx loveni 45
Atlantis, lost island of 55
Atlantis II 47
atoll 23, 24, 66, 70
Atolla 43
Autosub 53

B

bacteria 41, 43, 46, 47, 60
barnacle 38, 55, 68;
 goose 38
bends, the 48
Bermuda Triangle 55
bioluminescence 41, 70
bird, sea 28, 29, 38, 40, 62
bivalve 34, 35, 70, 71
blue-striped snapper 36
Botticelli, Sandro 16
*Branchiocerianthus
 imperator* 11
brittle star 6, 10, 45
bryozoan 20
buoy, monitoring 13
butterfly blenny 18

C

cable, underwater 44, 52
cephalopod 32, 70, 71
Challenger, HMS 11, 52
Chelonia mydas 39
clam 16–17, 18, 24, 30,
 34, 46–47, 58, 59;
 sand gaper 17
climate 12–13, 26, 66, 67
coastal waters 14–15, 18
cockle, heart 62
cod 57, 66
continental drift 7, 70; shelf
 8–10, 14, 70;slope 10, 70

copepod 27, 70, 71
coral 7, 10, 20, 22–25,
 62–63; black 22; brain 10,
 23; dead man's fingers 20;
 fire 22; gorgonian 23, 25;
 hydro- 22; organ-pipe 23;
 polyp 22–23, 71; reef
 22–25, 29, 54–55, 62;
 rose 23; sea fan 22–23
Coriolis Force 12
crab 16, 17, 21, 26–27,
 30–31; hermit 30–31;
 masked 17; pea 21;
 spider 21
crinoid 7
crustacean 18, 27, 30,
 38, 58, 70
current 12, 38, 66, 70

DE

Darwin, Charles 23
dead man's fingers 20
decompression 48, 61
Deep Star 53
defence 30–33
diatom 26, 70
diver 48–49, 50–51, 53,
 54, 61
diving bell 48; suit 49, 61
dolphin 27, 37;
 bottlenose 37
Dreadnought, HMS 51
dugong 16, 66
earthquake 45, 55, 67
echinoderm 19, 25, 70
eel 38, 42; gulper 10, 42
Euplectella aspergillium
 45
exploration, underwater
 52–53

FG

feather star 19
fish, angler- 10, 43;
 clown 24; craw- 18;
 cuttle- 30, 32;
 deep-sea 42–43;
 emperor angel- 25;
 flat 14; flying 10, 36, 64;
 grouper 53, 64; hatchet 10,
 40, 41; lancet 40–41;
 lantern 43; lion- 32;
 puffer 57; porcupine 64;
 rat-tail 10; red band 16;
 sargassum 30;
 stargazer 65; stone- 32;
 tripod 10; viper 40;
 weever 14; wolf 28;
 wrasse 64

fishing 26, 56–58, 66
flounder 14
food chain 70
food web 70
fossil 6–7; fuel 60–61
Gigantura 42–43
GLORIA 52
Great Barrier Reef 23
Gulf Stream 66

HIJ

Halley, Edmund 48
hurricane 12, 70
hydroid 21; giant 11
ice 11, 67; fast 11; pack 11
iceberg 11, 54, 67, 70
jellyfish 28, 32, 33, 41, 43,
 68; box 33; glass 41
jet propulsion 34–35

KL

Kaiko 66
kelp 11, 20–21
Kraken 34
lagoon, formation of 23
lateral lines 42
leafy sea dragon 8
Leptocephalus 38
lettuce slug 24–25
light organs 40–42
lobster 18–19, 30, 58;
 spiny 18
lumpsucker 20

M

mackerel 10, 65
maerl 32
man-of-war 10, 38
Mariana Trench 9, 47,
 53, 66
Melanocetus 43
Mid-Atlantic Ridge 9,
 46–47, 66
Mola mola 65
mollusc 34, 58, 71
monster, sea 19, 33, 34, 42
mother-of-pearl 58, 59
mussel 20–21, 59;
 date 25; horse 21

NO

Nautile 54–55
nautilus 37, 62–63
Neptune 9
Newt suit 61

Niño, El 63, 70
oarweed 10
Ocean, Arctic 8, 64, 67;
 Atlantic 7–9, 13–14,
 26, 38, 39, 41, 44, 55, 64,
 66; Indian 7–8, 24, 39, 41,
 63, 64, 66, 67; Pacific 8,
 11–12, 20, 24, 33, 39, 41,
 47, 64, 66; Southern 8,
 66, 67
octopus 10, 32, 34–35, 68;
 blue-ringed 32
oil and gas 60–61
Opisthoproctus 41
orange sea fan 22
overfishing 57, 66
oyster 59

PR

Palaeocoma 6
Panama Canal 66
Pangaea 7
Panthalassa 7
pearl 55, 59
Persian Gulf 64, 67
piddock 18
plankton 26–27, 28,
 64, 71; phytoplankton
 26, 28, 64, 67, 71;
 zooplankton 26–27,
 64, 71
plant 10, 16, 26
plate, crustal 9, 46;
 Caribbean 9;
 North American 9
Plateau, Guiana 8
plesiosaur 7
pollution 62, 66–67
polyp 20–23, 71
prawn 27, 29
predator 14, 18, 24–25,
 28–29, 30, 32, 33, 36, 40,
 41, 42–43
pycnogonid 44
ray 17, 33, 36–37, 65;
 blue-spotted 33;
 eagle 17;
 electric 36–37;
 reptile 7
rock 18–20, 46, 60

S

salmon 38, 56–57
salmon farming 56
salt 8–9, 11, 59, 65;
 farms 59
scallop 34, 35;
 queen 23
Scotoplanes 44

SCUBA diving 48, 50,
 52–53
Sea, Arabian 8, 67;
 Baltic 8, 66; Bering 8, 66;
 Caribbean 8–9, 41, 66;
 Coral 8, 66; Dead 9;
 Mediterranean 8, 59,
 66; North 60, 66;
 Red 8, 25, 50, 53, 63, 67;
 Sargasso 8, 38, 66;
 Tasman 8, 66;
 Tethys 7
sea 8–9, 71;
 bed 16–17, 44–45,
 54–55; cucumber 10,
 25, 44, 58; fan 22–23;
 fir 11, 21; grass 16, 58;
 lily 7, 19, 45; mat 20, 29;
 mouse 14; otter 11, 20,
 66, 69; pen 10, 16, 44,
 45; potato 17; slug 20,
 24–25; snail 30, 31, 47,
 58–59; snake 7; spider 10,
 44; urchin 11, 17, 18–19,
 29, 58
seahorse 17
seal 36, 38; harbour 36;
 elephant 36
seaweed 14, 20–21, 28,
 29, 30, 32, 58
sediment 9, 71
shark 10–11, 29, 62, 65;
 basking 29; cat 10–11;
 great white 62, 64;
 tiger 29; whale 65
shell 30–33, 59, 62–63, 68;
 gaping file 33;
 noble pen 59
shipwreck 54–55
shrimp 27, 47, 58
Siebe, Augustus 49
siphonophore 38
slate-pencil urchin 58
smoker, black 46–47, 70
snorkelling 50, 53, 69
sockeye salmon 57
sonar location 50, 52,
 56, 70
sponge 10, 44–45, 58, 63;
 basket 63;
 glass-rope 44;
 Venus flower-basket
 45
squid 10, 32, 34, 40,
 58
starfish 10, 19, 25;
 Bloody Henry 10;
 crown-of-thorns 25
Sternoptyx 41
submarine 50–51
submersible 47, 50–55,
 66, 71
sunstar 10; purple 19

TUV

temperature 8, 10, 13, 63,
 64, 66
tidal waves 45
tides 10, 64, 71
Titanic 54
Tolossa 55
trade winds 12, 66
trawler, fishing 57
treasure 54–55
trenches 8–10, 45
trilobite 7
tsunami 45, 71
Turtle 50
turtle 7, 10, 32, 38–39, 62;
 green 39, 67
typhoon 12, 71
underwater exploration
 48–55
Urashima Taro 39
vents 46–47;
 Galapagos 47
volcano 23, 45, 46

WZ

water spout 12
wave 12–13, 45, 65
weather 12–13
whale 10, 26, 27, 28, 36, 37,
 38, 40, 51, 62–63, 69;
 blue 36, 64, 65;
 humpback 28, 69;
 killer 27; sperm 10, 40, 51
whipnose 42
wind 12–13
Wiwaxia 6
wolf fish 28
worm 14–15, 55; bristle
 14; parchment 15;
 peacock 14–15; peanut 14;
 tube 15, 46, 47
zone, dark 10, 42, 43,
 70;fracture 9; sunlit 10,
 64, 71;
 twilight 10, 40–41, 71

Acknowledgements

Dorling Kindersley would like to thank:
for their invaluable assistance during
photography: The University Marine Biological
Station, Scotland, especially Prof. Johon
Davenport, David Murden, Bobbie Wilkie,
Donald Patrick, Phil Lonsdale, Ken Cameron,
Dr. Jason Hall-Spencer, Simon Thurston, Steve
Parker, Geordie Campbell, and Helen Thirlwall;
Sea Life Centres (UK), especially Robin James,
David Copp, Patrick van der Menve, and Ian
Shaw (Weymouth); and Marcus Goodsir
(Portsmouth); Colin Pelton, Peter Hunter, Dr.
Brian Bett, and Mike Conquer of the Institute of
Oceanographic Sciences;Tim Parmenter, Simon
Caslaw, and Paul Ruddock of the Natural
History Museum, London; Margaret Bidmead of
the Royal Navy Submarine Museum, Gosport;
IFREMER for their kind permission to
photograph the model of *Nautile*; David Fowler
of Deep Sea Adventure; Mak Graham, Andrew
and Richard Pierson of Otterferry Salmon Ltd;
Bob Donalson of Angus Modelmakers; Sally

Rose for additional research; Kathy Lockley for
providing props; Helena Spiteri, Djinn von
Noorden, Susan St. Louis, Ivan Finnegan, Joe
Hoyle, Mark Haygarth, and David Pickering for
editorial and design assistance; David Ekholm–
JAlbum, Sunita Gahir, Susan St. Louis, Carey
Scott, Lisa Stock, and Bulent Yusuf for the
clipart; Neville Graham, Sue Nicholson, and
Susan St. Louis for the wallchart; Trevor Day
for his assistance on the paperback edition.

**For this relaunch edition, the publisher would
also like to thank:** Camilla Hallinan for text
editing, and Carron Brown for proofreading.

The publisher would like to thank the following
for their kind permission to reproduce their
photographs:

a=above, b=below, c=center, l=left, r=right, t=top
Alamy Images: Paul Glendell 60tr; **American
Museum of Natural History:** 11tl (no. 419(2));

Heather Angel 38bc; **Ardea**/Val Taylor 62 cr;
Tracy Bowden/Pedro Borrell: 55 tc; **Bridgeman
Art Library**/Prado, Madrid 9tr; Uffizi Gallery,
Florence 16tr' Bruce Coleman Ltd/Carl
Roessler 22c, Frieder Sauer 26tr, Charles &
Sandra Hood 27tc, Jeff Foott 28tr, 56tr, Jane
Burton 38bl, Michael Roggo 57tr Orion service
& Trading Co. 58br, Atlantide SDF 59tr, Nancy
Selton 63br, to Library: 7br; **Steven J. Cooling**
60br; **Corbis:** Jerome Sessini 60–61b, Ralph
White 67c, 71bc, Roger Wood 67tr, Tom
Stewart 66br; **The Deep, Hull:** Craig Stennet/
Guzelian 68cr; **Mary Evans Picture Library**
11tr, 12tr, 19tl, 20tl, 28tl, 33tr, 34tr, 40cl. 45tr,
48tr, 49tl, 50bl, 52tr. 54c; **Getty Images:**
Nikolas Konstatinou 69tl, Will & Den McIntype
66bl; **Ronald Grant Archive** 42cl, 55bl; **Robert
Harding Picture Library** 25tl, 32tr, 32bc,
39br, 57tr, 63tl; **Institute of Oceanographic
Sciences:** 46lc; **Jamstec:** 66cl; © **Japanese
Meteorological Agency**/Meteorological Office
12l; **Frank Lane Photo Agency**/M. Neqwman
11br; **Simon Conway Moiris:** 6tr; **N.H.P.A.**/
Agence natur 44c, Linda and Brian Pitkin 67tl,
Peter Parks 64bl; **National Oceanography
Centre, Southampton:** 46lc; **Nature Picture
Library:** David Shale 70tl, Doc White 65b, Fabio
Liverani 65tr, leff Foott 69cl, Jurgen Freund

64–65, Peter Scoones 65cl, Thomas D.
Mangelsen 69b; **Oxford Scientific Films**/toi de
Roy 29t, Fred Bavendam 43 tl, David Cayless
68bl, 68–69, Howard Hall 64rr, Rick Price/SAL
67b, Scott Winer 70–71; **Planet Earth Pictures**/
Peter Scoones 9tl, Norbert Wu 10–11c, 20cl,
40tr, 40tl, 4lt, 42tr, Gary Bell 23br, 55tr, Mark
Conlin 25c, 36br, Menuhin 29tc, Ken Lucas
30tl, NevilJe Coleman 33cr, Steve Bloom 37c,
Andrew Mounter 38br, Larry Madin 43 br, Ken
Vaughari 51 cr, Georgette Doowma 63cr;
Science Photo Library/Dr. G. Feldman 26bl,
Ron Church 53 cr, Douglas Faulkner 66cr,
Simon Fraser 62bl, NASA/Goddard Space
Flight Centre 70br, Tom Van Sant, Geosphere
Project/Planetary, Visions 64cl; **Frank Spooner
Pictures:** 47tr, 47cr, 54br, 54bl, 60bl, 61tr; **Tony
Stone Images:** Jeff Rotman 53lc; **Stoll Comex
Seaway Ltd:** 61tl; **Town Cocks Museum:** Hull
63tr; **ZEFA:** 36cl, 56ct.

Wallchart credits:
Corbis: Gary Bell; zefa cl (shoal); Martin
Harvey/ Gallo Images br (oil spill).

All other images © Dorling Kindersley.
For further information see:
www.dkimages.com